Massacre My Heart

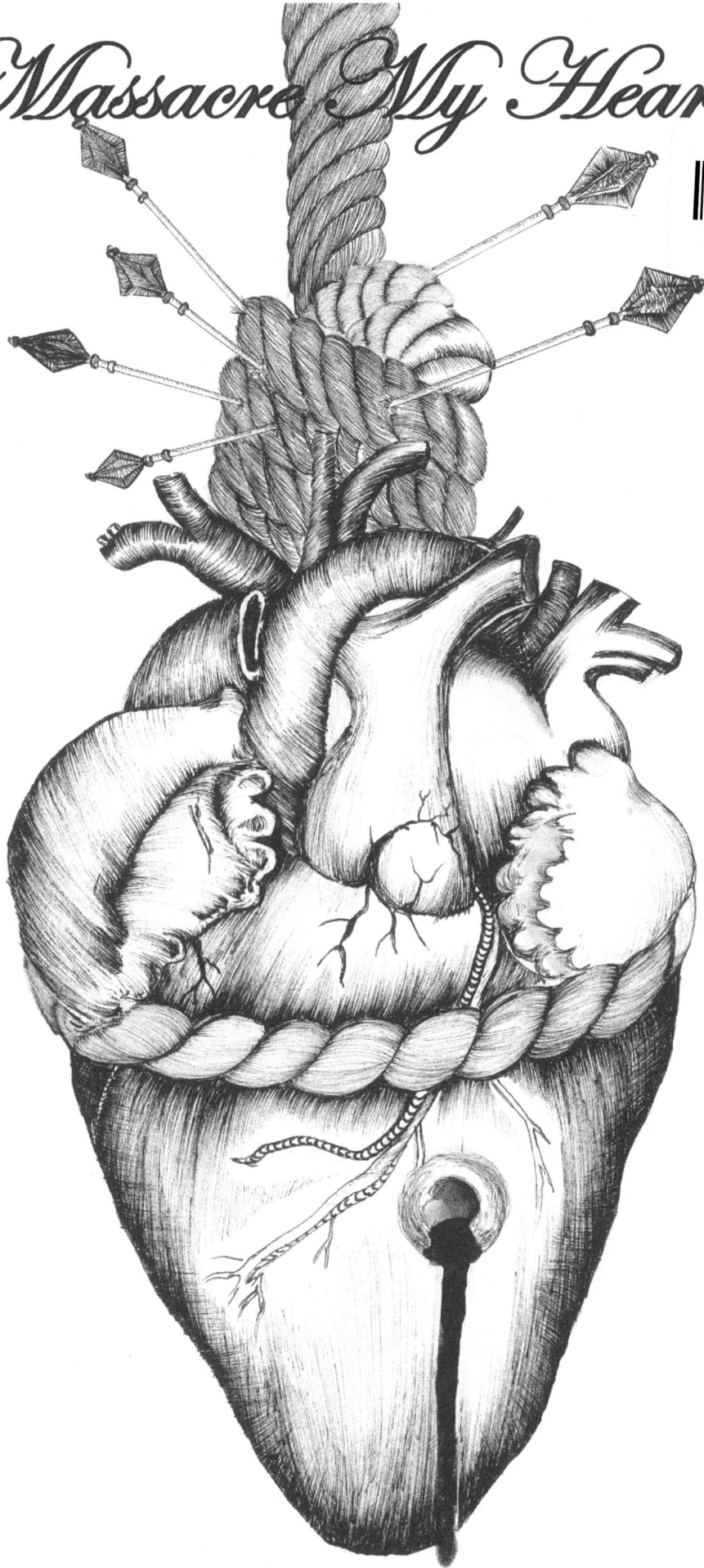

By: Scarlet Wyvern

I0159046

Massacre My Heart

By: Scarlet Wyvern

Copyright © 2019 Scarlet Wyvern.

To my mother, Donna, who carried me through the storm that raged inside me.

To Jen Woolley and The Bucks County Writers Group for their love and support.

To Jace, who stole my heart with his first kick. The world grew brighter the day you were born.

And to anyone struggling against their inner demons. You are stronger than you know. You are loved. You are not alone.

Table Of Contents

Table Of Contents

Table Of Contents

Table Of Contents

Unsteady

This depression is oppressive

And it makes me unsteady

But I try to move forward

Though my heart weighs me down

Like an anchor

This whole ships gonna drown

And my soul is just a fragment of what it used to be

Cause I've lost so many pieces

to the predator's jaws

Those whose problems

I thought I could solve

Be their messiah

Their desire

nailed me to the cross

So I'm holding tight to the lifeline you threw me

But still I'm chocking on the waves

Drowning on my own broken heart

I'm clinging to you tightly

As I tear apart

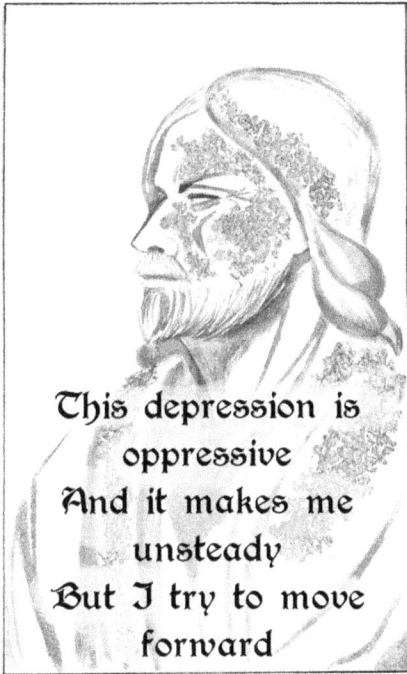

This depression is oppressive
And it makes me unsteady
But I try to move forward

Though my heart weighs me down
Like an anchor
This whole ships gonna drown
And my soul is just a fragment of what it used to be
Cause I've lost so many pieces to the predator's jaws

Those whose problems I thought I could solve

Be there messiah
Their desire
Nailed me to the cross
So I'm holding tight to the life line you threw me
But still I'm chocking on the waves
Drowning on my own broken heart

I'm clinging to you tightly
As I tear apart

9

Dear Darling

Dear darling
You're dead now
So I guess you'll never get
This letter
Remember when we met at the bar
Thought I'd never see you smile
My heart burns for your smile
Even if you're a million miles away
Under the soil
Burning at the core
Crawling with worms
It breaks my heart to think about it

Dear darling
How's purgatory treating you
Maybe I should pray for you
You were right about the bridge being out
I was right to hold my tongue
And if I never see you again
I promise I'll never forget
The look on your face
As we tumbled into the river
And oh the sound that was almost a scream
And how I thought I'd never see you smile
Again

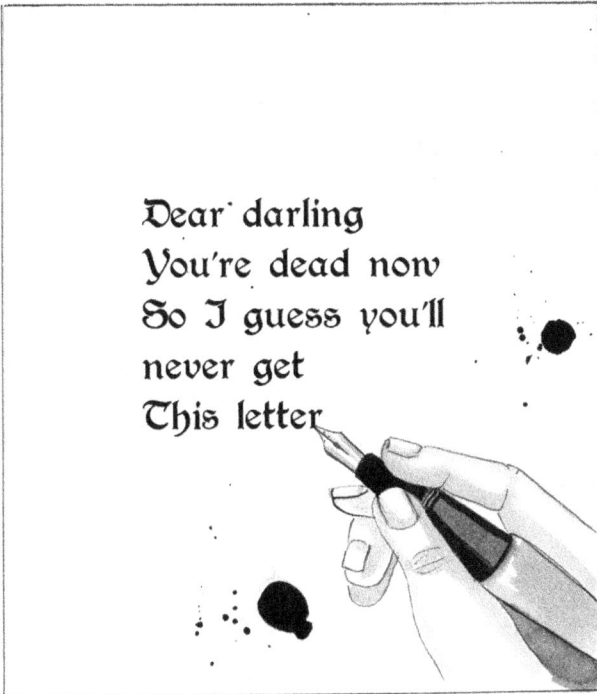

Dear darling
You're dead now
So I guess you'll
never get
This letter

Remember when we met at the bar
Thought I'd never see you smile
My heart burns for your smile

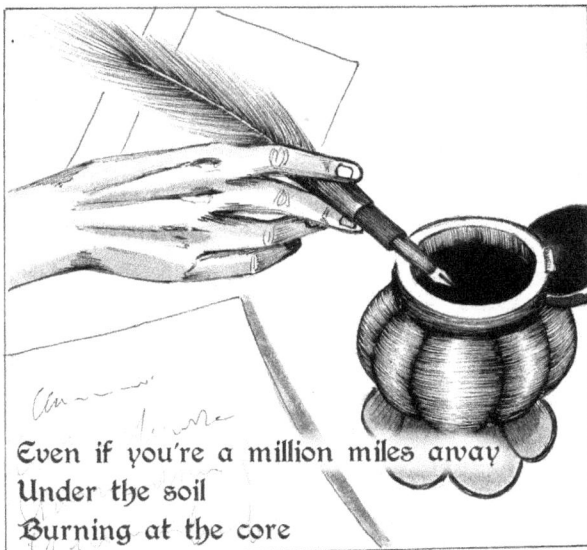

Even if you're a million miles away
Under the soil
Burning at the core

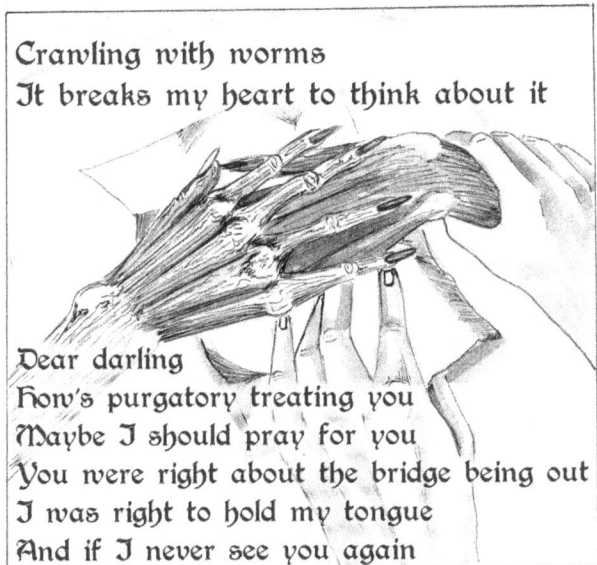

Crawling with worms
It breaks my heart to think about it

Dear darling
How's purgatory treating you
Maybe I should pray for you
You were right about the bridge being out
I was right to hold my tongue
And if I never see you again

I promise I'll never forget
The look on your face
As we tumbled into the river
And oh the sound that was almost
a scream
And how I thought I'd never see
you smile
Again

Erupting In Darkness

Erupting in darkness

Your hollow eyes

Bound by what you left behind

Tethered to an empty void

The vessel that you once employed

Try to flee

I wish I might

Intoxicated

By your absence of light

Hallowed darkness spreads

Through your veins

Extinguishing the spark in me

I suppose there is no worse hell

Then sitting in a room with the empty shell

Of the person, I used to love so well

Erupting in darkness
Your hollow eyes
Bound by what you left behind
Tethered to an empty void

The vessel that you once employed
Try to flee
I wish I might
Intoxicated
By your absence of light

Hallowed darkness spreads
Through your veins
Extinguishing the spark in me
I suppose there is no worse hell
Then sitting in a room with the
empty shell
Of the person I used to love so well

We All Fall

Misused

Mistrusted

Broken, beat, and lied to

Tied too

A life of limitations

Facing down the demons

Feeling kinda squeamish

Think we don't have feelings

Healing never happens

Hearts harden

Morals slacken

Trade it

Berate it

Bearer of the whip

Snaps

Collapse

Take another

Kill now

Breathing in

Never out

Greedy

Needy

Everyone had better please me

Tease me

Fake it

Take it

Try

You'll never make it

Burn sweet

 The heat

Prickling on my skin

Stab me straight through

The monster I turned you into

A cycle the world can cling to

Darkening

Hardening

Our very existence

One by one

We all fall

We

All

Fall

Misused
Mistrusted
Broken, beat, and lied to
Tied too
A life of limitations

Facing down the demons
Feeling kinda squeamish
Think we don't have feelings
Healing never happens

Hearts harden
Morals slacken
Trade it
Berate it

Bearer of the whip
Snaps
Collapse
Take another
Kill now
Breathing in
Never out

Greedy
Needy
Everyone had better please me
Tease me
Fake it
Take it
Try
You'll never make it
Burn sweet
The heat
Prickling on my skin
Stab me straight through
The monster I turned you into

A cycle the world can cling to
Darkening
Hardening
Our very existence

One by one
We all fall
We
All
Fall

An Apple A Day

An Apple A Day
  Keeps The Doctor Away
  But Sometimes
  Its The Doctor You Need

Eggshells

What's a life on eggshells
  Every step I take
I'm standing on thin ice
Waiting for it to break
I'm sinking in quicksand
No one can hear me scream
They're all screaming at me
The eggshells crack beneath my feet
And with each step another mistake
And with each crack, another layer of eggshells lays beneath my feet
And with each layer of eggshells, a tear slides down my face
I live a life on eggshells
I cannot escape

What's a life on eggshells
Every step I take
I'm standing on thin ice
Waiting for it to break

I'm sinking in quicksand
No one can hear me scream
They're all screaming at me

The eggshells crack beneath my feet
And with each step another mistake

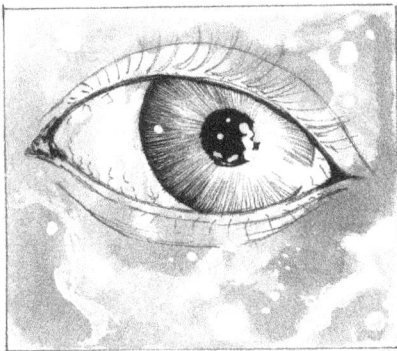

And with each crack, another layer of eggshells lays beneath my feet
And with each layer of eggshells, a tear slides down my face
I live a life on eggshells
I cannot escape

Despair

The halo you wear is tinted gray
Fellow brethren, despair is settling upon us
Winding roots of agony
Blur the optical illusions
Realization that truth is undeniable
And hide able are we
And deniable faith
Is just tearing up on your face
The resemblance of the truth
We find in lies
Only pollution in our eyes
And when faced with the truth, my sisters
We are faced with despair
And we knew it was coming
My brothers, it's just a matter of time
Before the lie becomes the truth

The halo you wear is tinted gray
Fellow brethren, despair is settling upon us
Winding roots of agony
Blur the optical illusions

Realization that truth is undeniable
And hide-able are we
And deniable faith
Is just tearing up on your face
The resemblance of the truth
We find in lies

Only pollution in our eyes
And when faced with the truth, my sisters
We are faced with despair

And we knew it was coming
My brothers, it's just a matter of time
Before the lie becomes the truth

Imaginary Friend

Looking at my bleeding wrists

I see

I was never more

Than a figment of your imagination

How dare you use me for your assassination

I'm only your imaginary friend

I only feel through your emotions

I know only what you say is real

But wrap my hands around your neck

Force me to squeeze

What else could I do

I live through you

How dare you use me for
Your assassination

Looking down at my bleeding wrists
I see
I was never more
Than a figment of your
Imagination

I'm only your
imaginary friend
I only feel
through your
emotions

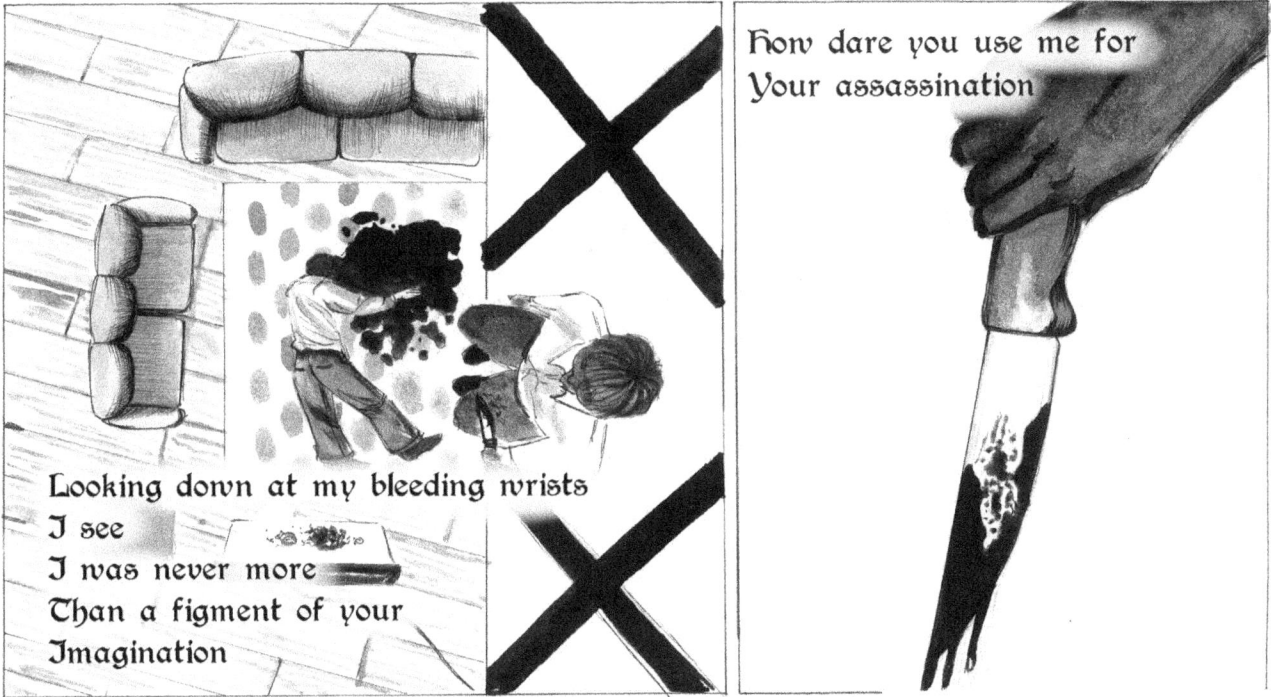

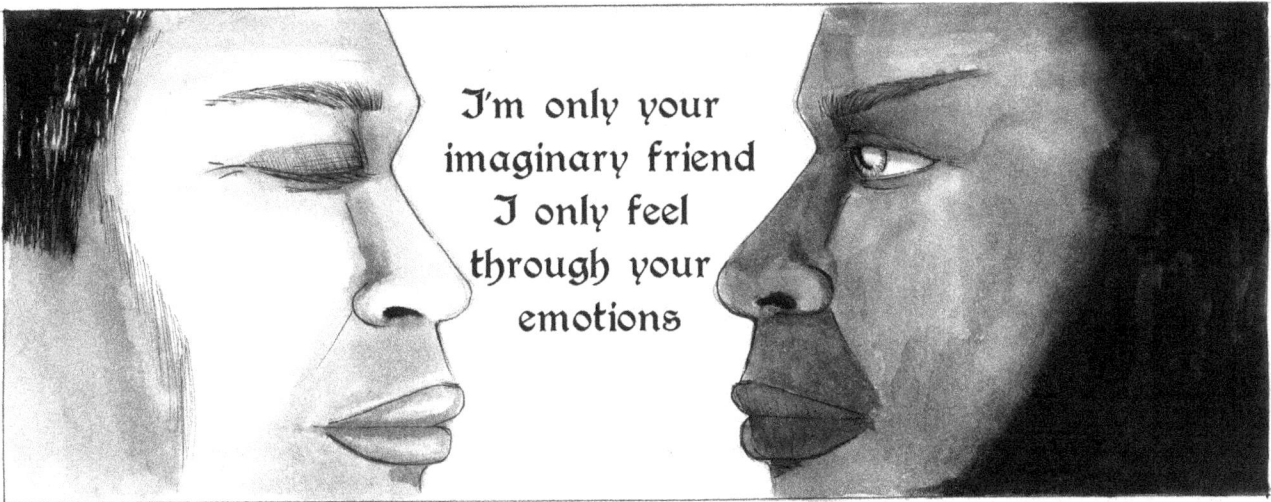

I know only what you say is real
But wrap my hands around your neck
Force me to squeeze
What else could I do
I live through you

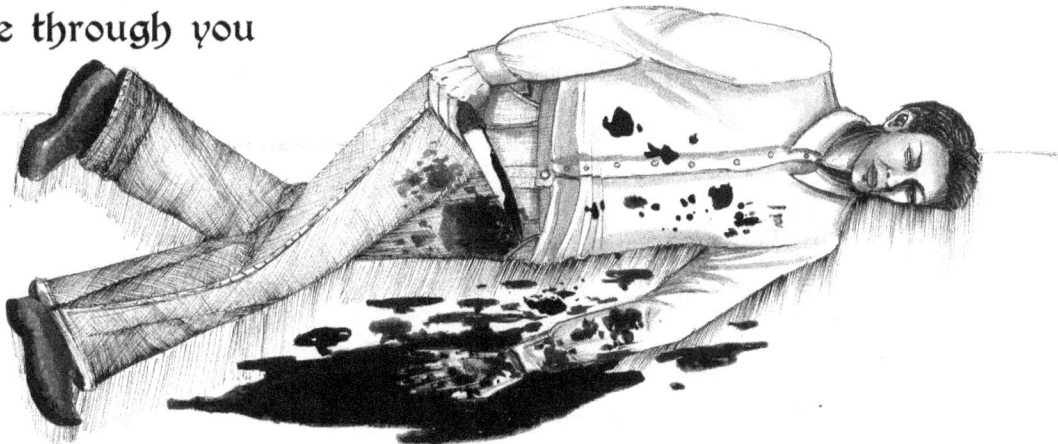

Her Precipice

She stood on the precipice

Of her own reflection

A growing Notion

Tries to hide from herself

Cold Anticipation

Knowing

Hate and Rejection

Were what was waiting

Should she chose to be herself

She Stood on the precipice
Of her own reflection
A growing notion
Tries to hide from herself
Cold anticipation
Knowing hate and rejection
Were what was waiting
If she chose to be herself

Bittersweet

Bittersweet

My love for the rose

The petals that please

A silky feel against my cheek

How they tickle my chin

Oh, the thorns

How they bite at my flesh

Surrounded by the encouraging beauty of the petals

And the sweet scent that drawls me in

Only to be pushed away by those damned thorns

To look longingly into my rose's eyes

And see thorns

Bittersweet
My love for the rose
The petals that please
A silky feel against my cheek

How they tickle my chin
Oh, the thorns
How they bite at my flesh

Surrounded by the encouraging beauty of the petals
And the sweet scent that draws me in

Only to be pushed away
by those damned thorns
To look longingly into my
rose's eyes
And see thorns

Spiderweb

Oh what a tangled web we weave

When first we practice to deceive

You got caught

Ensnared in your own foolish plot

To face the devils

You have wrought

For when you bite the hand that feeds

It may reach out and

Hold you by the throat

To choke the life from traitorous foe

Oh what a tangled web you wove

No longer the spider

You are the flea

And now this web belongs to me

Oh what a tangled web
we weave
When first we practice to
deceive

You got caught
ensnared in your own
foolish plot
To face the devils
you have wrought

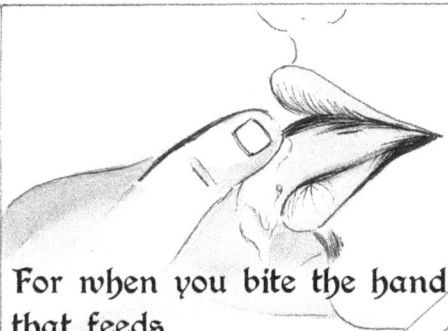

For when you bite the hand
that feeds
It may reach out
and
hold you by
the throat

to choke the life
from traitorous foe
Oh tangled in the web you wove
No longer the spider
You are the flea

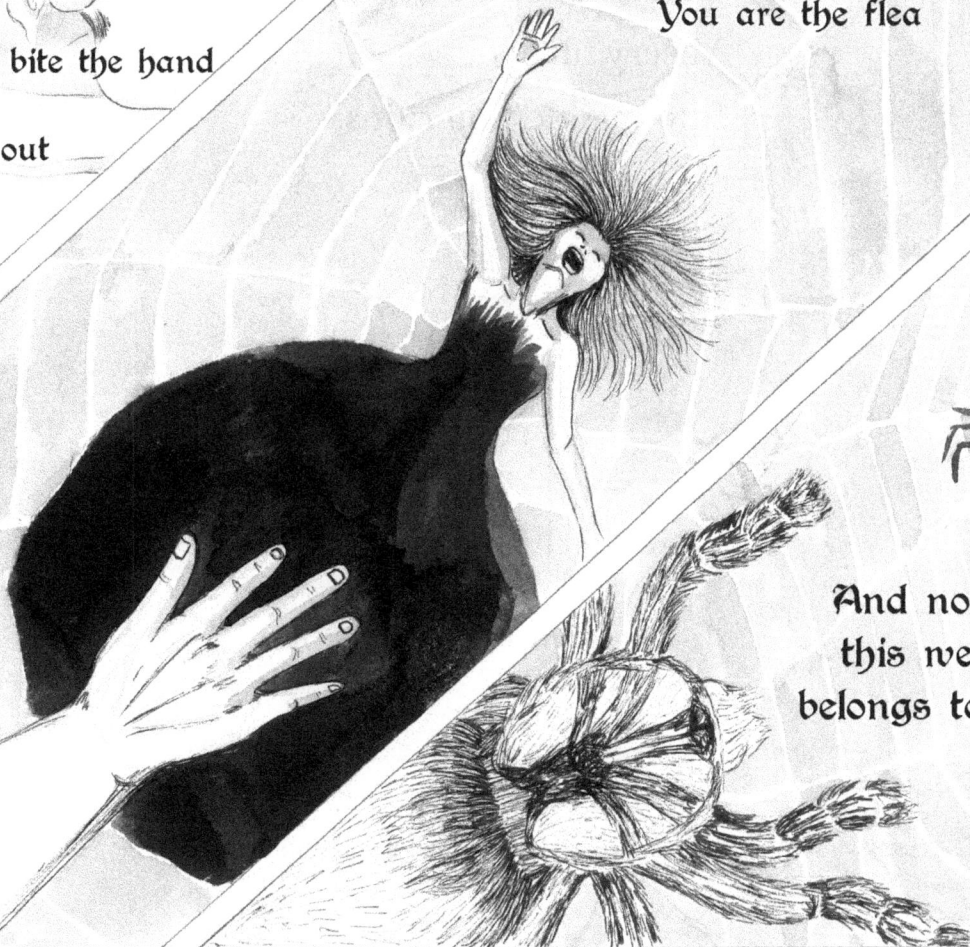

And now
this web
belongs to me

Misery

Misery

Rendered polite

Hidden the savage

Deep in the eyes

Were it something wrong

That none could assuage

Misery turns

Into maddening ruins

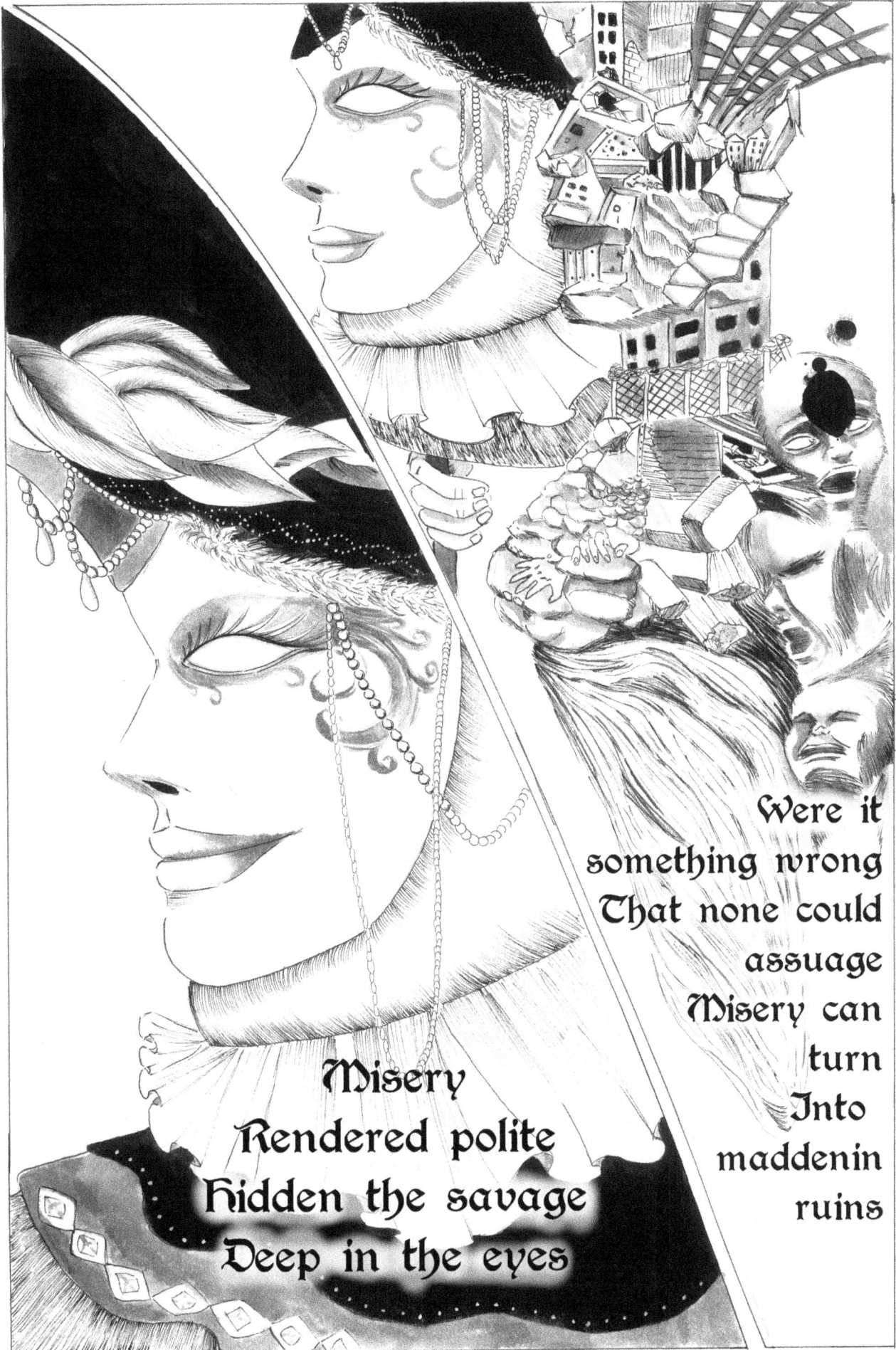

Misery
Rendered polite
Hidden the savage
Deep in the eyes

Were it
something wrong
That none could
assuage
Misery can
turn
Into
maddenin
ruins

The Razor

I was everything you needed

a rock

 a shoulder

one to hold you in your hours of need

I thought you were pure

But I know

I am the better of our two souls

When I tried to pull you up

You laughed and dragged me down

to hell

I am a failing savior

Trying to save those that are beyond redemption

Save your soul

Breaking mine

But You are the bullet

You are the gun

Your voice is poison

Your heart is numb

You are the dark

the darkness of the room

that scares a young child

You know you are my doom

You are the razor

At my wrist

I hate you

But goddamn I love you

So cut

You cut

You cut

You cut me

Peirce my flesh

Set the blood free

Why did I

Why did I

Pick you up

All you do is cut

I set you down, and I miss you

I pick you up, and you break me

You are the darkness I crave

I held you up

You pulled me down

Focused so hard on saving

Now I've fallen

And I see

There is no hand for me to reach

So Bravo

Encore

Come on Break me again

Use me

See how much you can make me bleed

Lie

Tell them all I'm your villain

I take the razor

I cut the veins

In my wrist

Tears well in my eyes
Congrats
I'm lying on the floor
My son just lost his mother
They lay me down
In the cold ground
And you have a new story to tell
Lie
Say you tried to save me
No
 NO
RAGE
You should feel this pain
I am the innocent
You are the monster
I was the prey
Now I got my silver bullets
And my wooden stake
I'm going to hunt you down
Go on twist them lies
Shoot you right between the eyes
Your baby boy will come to hate you
Like they all do
I Will Burn You Down
I Will
Burn You
To The Ground

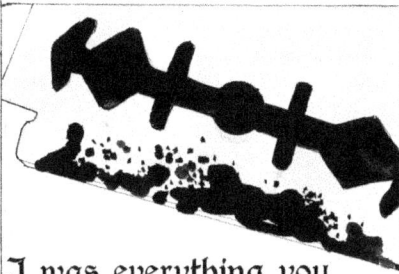

I was everything you
needed
A rock
 A shoulder
One to hold you in your
hours of need
I thought you were
pure
But I know
I am the better of our
two souls
When I tried to pull you
up
You laughed and
dragged me down
to hell
I am a failing savior
Trying to save those
that are beyond
redemption
Save your soul
Breaking mine
But, You are the bullet
You are the gun
Your voice is poison
Your heart is numb
You are the dark
The darkness of the
room
that scares a young child
You know you are my
doom

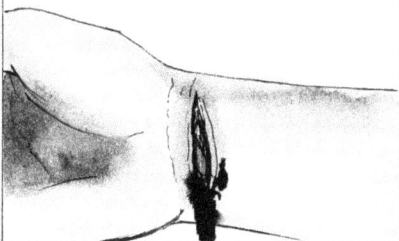

You are the razor
At my wrist
I hate you
But goddamn I love you
So cut
You cut
You cut
You cut me
Pierce my flesh
Set the blood free
Why did I
Why did I
Pick you up
All you do is cut
I set you down and I
miss you
I pick you up and you
break me
You are the darkness I
crave
I held you up
You pulled me down
Focused so hard on
saving
Now I've fallen
And I see
There is no hand for me
to reach
So Bravo
Encore
Come on Break me again
Use me
See how much you can
make me bleed
Lie
Tell them all I'm your
villain

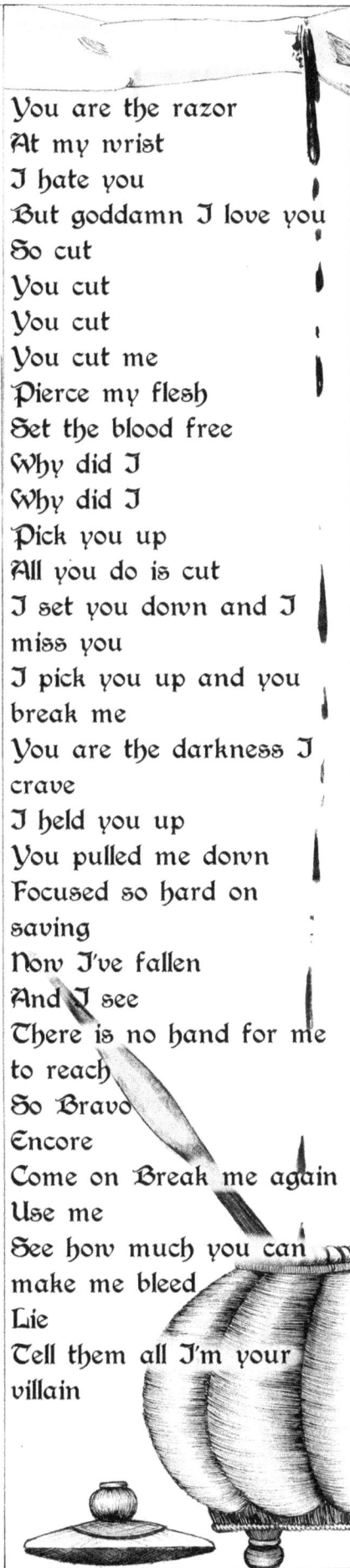

I take the razor
I cut the veins
In my wrist
Tears well in my eyes
Congrats
I'm lying on the floor
My son just lost his mother
They lay me down
In the cold ground
And you have a new story
to tell
Lie
Say you tried to save me
No
 no
Rage
You should feel this pain
I am the innocent
You are the monster
I was the prey
Now I got my silver bullets
And my wooden stake
I'm going to hunt you down
Go on twist them lies
Shoot you right between
the eyes
Your baby boy will come to
hate you
Like they all do
I Will Burn You Down
I Will
Burn You
To The Ground

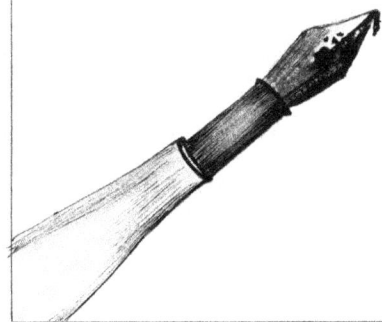

35

Tommy

Everyone says
You'll be alright
But they're just hoping
Wishful thinking
No one knows
If it were me
In your shoes
So many things
I'd have to do
Like bungee jumping
Riding a motorcycle
Saying whatever I feel
The white blood cells
Fight hard
Little soldiers
But if they were to lose
I'd regret what I never did
And you in your shoes
So content
With water guns
And bowling
I wonder if you worry
About losing to the cancer
I hope you're not so good
Cause I once heard
That God only takes you when you're young
If you're good

Everyone says
You'll be alright
But they're just hoping
Wishful thinking
No one knows
If it were me
In your shoes

So many things
I'd have to do
Like bungee jumping
Riding a motorcycle
Saying whatever I feel

The white blood cells
Fight hard
Little soldiers
But if they were to lose
I'd regret what I never did
And you in your shoe

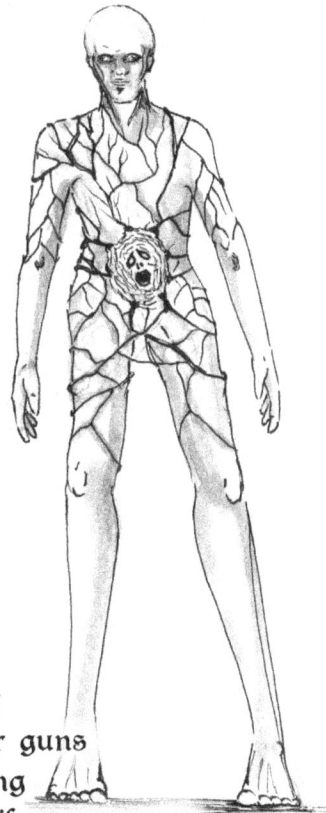

So content
With water guns
And bowling
I wonder if you worry
About losing to the cancer
I hope you're not so good
Cause I once heard
That God only takes you when you're young
If you're good

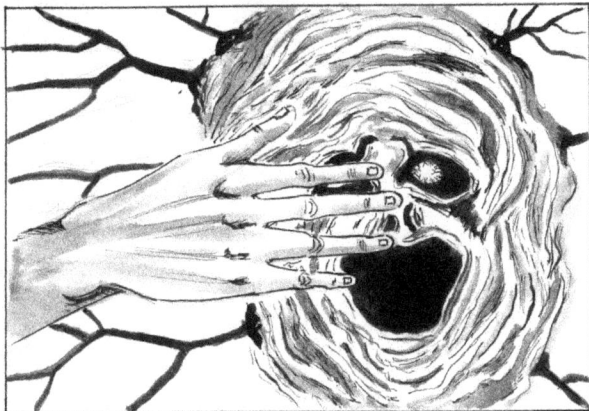

37

Feelings After

Where you dwell
I cannot follow
Where you are
I cannot know
I Know that heaven
Bares no sorrow
We hold it all within our hearts
Did you hear the angels singing
When they came to take your soul
Was it a joy or it a burden
To die that January, cold

Where you dwell
I cannot follow
Where you are
I cannot know

I Know that heaven
Bares no sorrow
We hold it all within our hearts
Did you hear the angels singing

When they came to take your soul
Was it a joy or it a burden
To die that January, cold

Harsh Truths

I will not murder
I will not maim
I will not give into
Hatred's game

I will pretend that you care
I will pretend
there's something there
I will pretend I am worth more
Then a speck of dust
upon the floor

I will not murder
I will not maim
I will not give into
Hatred's game

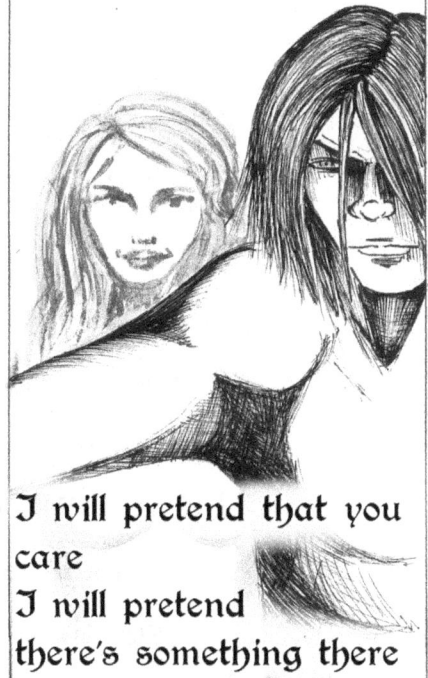

I will pretend that you
care
I will pretend
there's something there

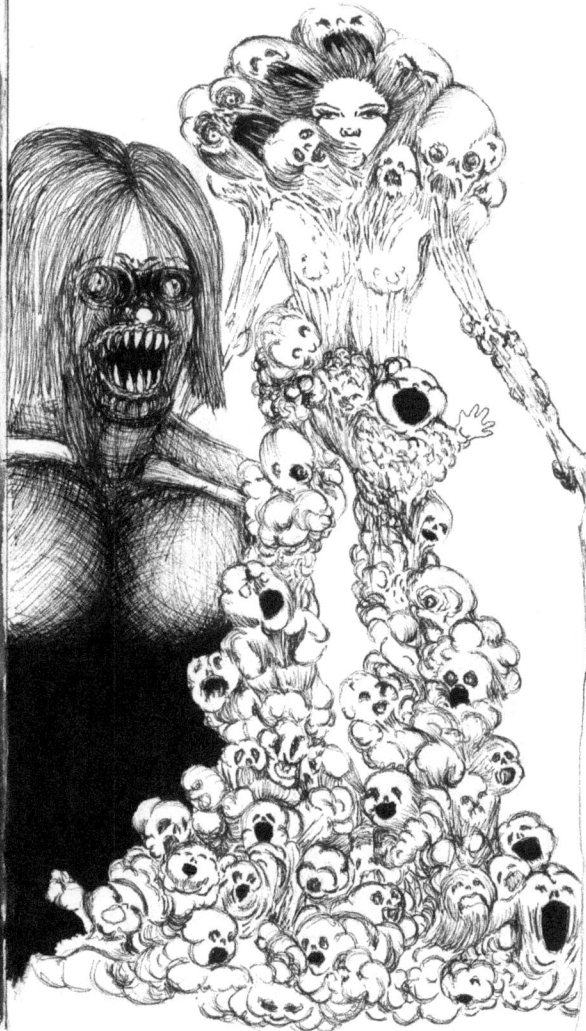

I will pretend I am
worth more
Then a speck of dust
Upon the floor

At Church

A chorus of hallelujahs

As I admit I am a scar

On the face of the virgin

Ten hail Mary's and two glory be's

Then I take my seat

He sits in the back pew with a gun in his hand

He kneels and prays and

Passes the gun to the girl beside him

Slowly

Over a hail of The Lord's prayer

The gun is passed forward

A boy passes me the gun

I pray and then cock it

I pass the gun on

Lastly, the gun is past to the priest

"Glory to God in the highest" he cries

And shoot the bible

He shoots the virgin and her son

He goes back to his sermon

But we all leave

Except for me

I go take the gun

I dip it in holy water

A chorus of hallelujahs
As I admit I am a scar
On the
Face of the virgin

Ten Hail Mary's
and two glory be's
Then I take my seat

He sits in the back pew
with a gun in his hand

He kneels and
prays and
Passes the gun to
the girl beside him
Slowly

Over a hail of The Lord's prayer
The gun is passed forward
A boy passes me the gun
I pray and then cock it
I pass the gun on
Lastly, the gun is passed to the priest

"Glory to God in the highest" he cries
And shoot the Bible
He shoots the virgin and her son
He goes back to his sermon

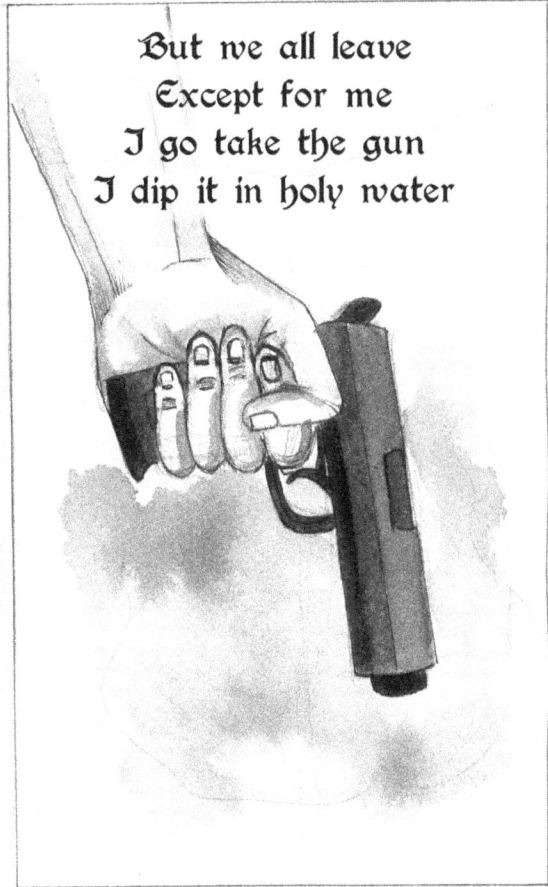

But we all leave
Except for me
I go take the gun
I dip it in holy water

The Trade

Her heart was laying upon the hearth

A thug came to find it and asked

"Is this yours?"

"Aye," she answers, "But it is too sweet."

"I wish for something bitter."

The thug in reply said "My heart is bitter and yours is sweet

Let us trade and bring us both peace."

"Ah," she said. "You will be heavily rewarded."

The thug ripped his heart out of his chest

The woman dipped it in vinegar and swallowed it whole

The woman then pushed the man into the fire

Over his dying screams, she said, "You have been heavily rewarded."

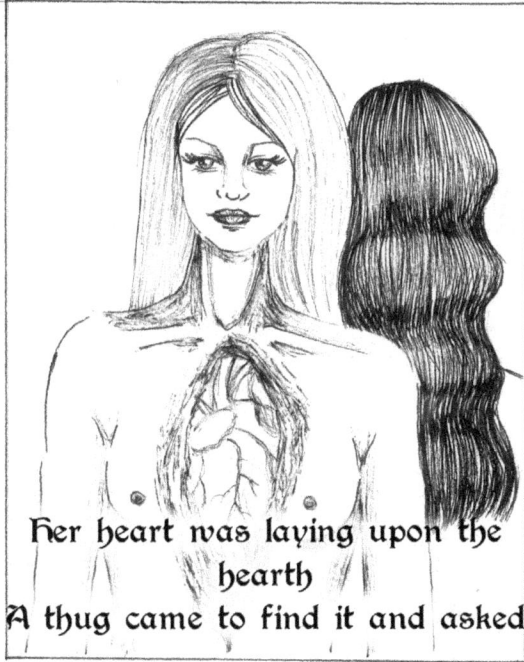

Her heart was laying upon the hearth
A thug came to find it and asked

"Is this yours?"
"Aye," she answers
"But it is too sweet."

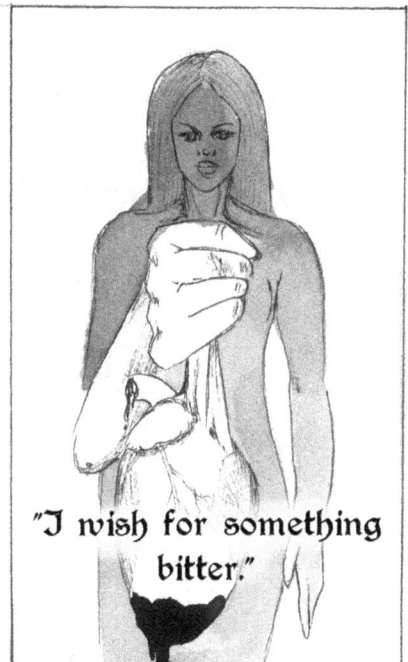

"I wish for something bitter."

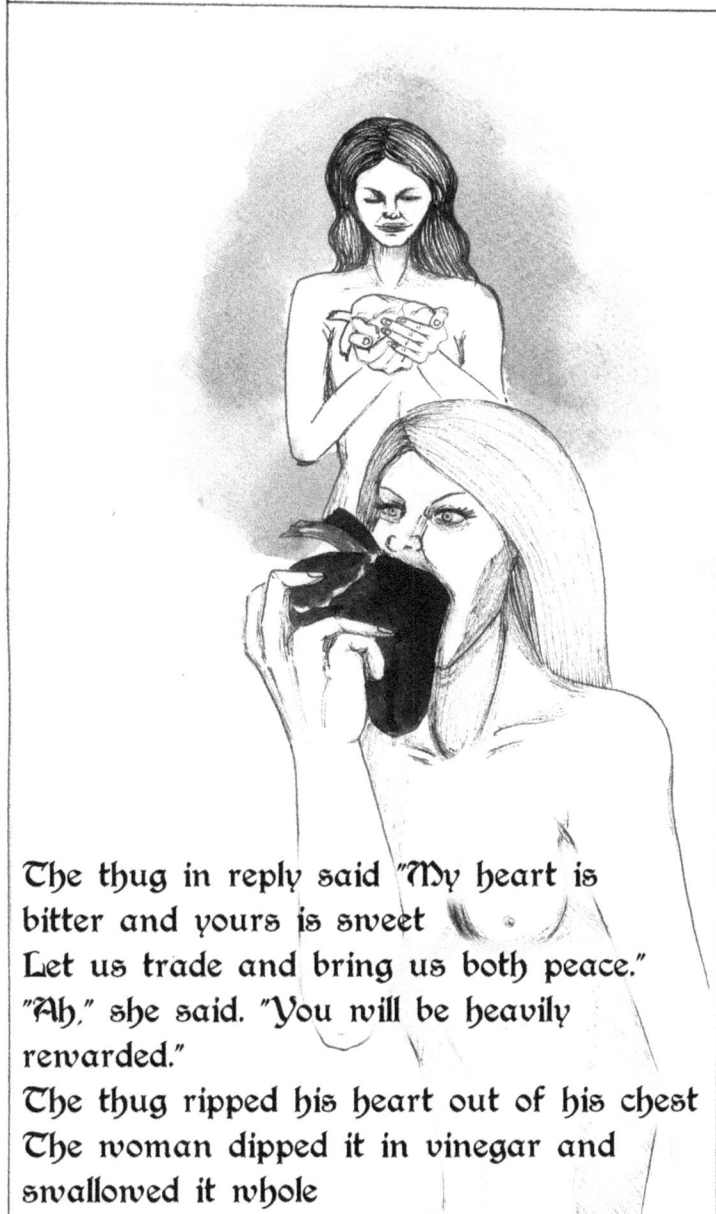

The thug in reply said "My heart is bitter and yours is sweet
Let us trade and bring us both peace."
"Ah," she said. "You will be heavily rewarded."
The thug ripped his heart out of his chest
The woman dipped it in vinegar and swallowed it whole

The woman then pushed the man into the fire
Over his dying screams, she said, "You have been heavily rewarded."

45

Society Of The Damned

Mimic me a world

Of peace

Tranquility

The outer edge of our society

Underneath the flesh

Lies the unexposed

Where daggers fly

Where the hungry beg

Where children lie down in their graves

Where life is no longer valued

The flesh is bleeding always

But still, it will conceal

No one wants to know the truth

Never will it heal

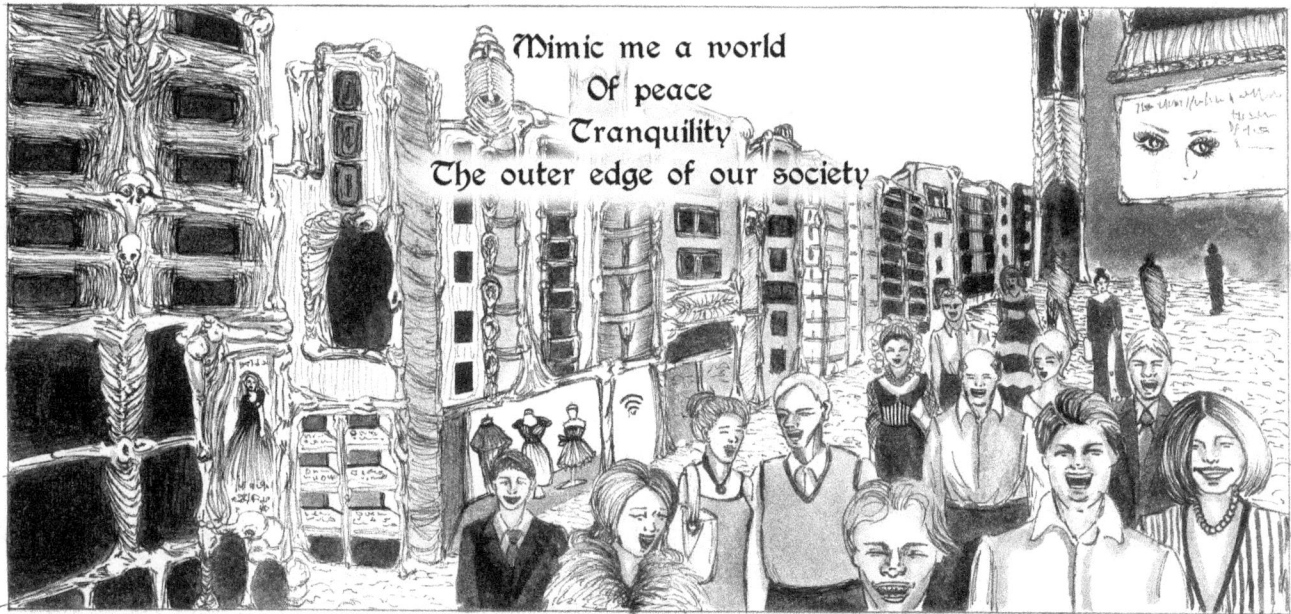

Mimic me a world
Of peace
Tranquility
The outer edge of our society

Underneath the flesh
Lies the unexposed
Where daggers fly
Where the hungry beg
Where children lie down in their graves

Where life is no longer valued
The flesh is bleeding always
But still, it will conceal
No one wants to know the truth
Never will it heal

All To Get To You

I crawled through the dirt

I slept in the rain

I fell in a ditch

I buried the pain

I drove heading south till that damn car broke down

I hitchhiked for hours

I stole away on a boat

And when I was found

I swam till I cramped

I thought I would drown

All of these things

All to get to you

But when I got to you

You were gone

I crawled through the dirt
I slept in the rain
I fell in a ditch
I buried the pain

I drove heading south till
that damn car broke down
I hitchhiked for hours

I stole away on a boat
And when I was found
I swam till I cramped
I thought I would drown

All of these things
All to get to you

But when I got to you
You were gone

Lust

Lust

A Dark desire

Temper me in scorching fire

Delightful pain

For which I aspire

Trembling with unhinged lust

Bait you

Waiting for your touch

Breath and whimper

Sweet melding bodies simmer

Rhythmic heartbeats

Soaring higher

Hypnotic dancing

We perspire

Ecstasy implodes

Inside her

Euphoria

Forged of carnal thirst

A rhapsidous crescendo

Inside of us

Burst

Trembling with unhinged lust
Bait you

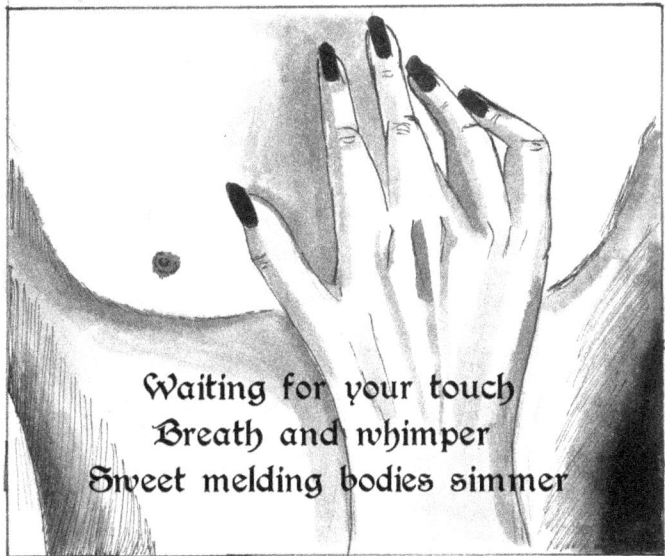

Lust
A Dark desire
Temper me in scorching fire
Delightful pain
For which I aspire

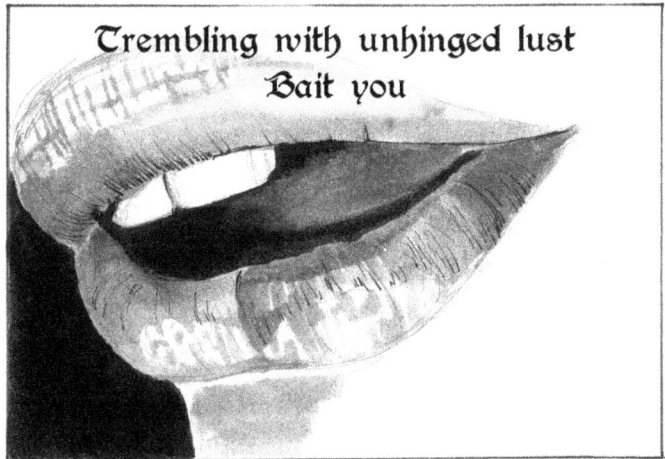

Waiting for your touch
Breath and whimper
Sweet melding bodies simmer

Rhythmic heartbeats
soaring higher
hypnotic dancing

We perspire
Ecstasy implodes
Inside her
Euphoria

Forged of carnal thirst
A rhapisodous
crescendo
Inside of us, bursts

I Hold Onto You So Tightly

I hold onto you so tightly

Because to let you go

Would tear free a storm inside me so violent

That I should be but ash

burnt upon the shores of its malevolence

I hold onto you so tightly
Because to let you go
would tear free a storm inside me so violent
That I should be but ash burnt upon the
shores of its malevolence

The Denial Of My Beating Heart

It is the Denial of my beating heart

the Denial of my breathing lungs

That brings me to my petulant tomb

where catatonic

I bare life

with no deliverance in sight

Dismissed is joy and revere

And blinded by the truth

In one town the apocalypse came

and shook the foundation to the ground

All began for

What I wanted most

Wasn't mine to take

But how could I refuse such lips

And ever such a fragrant kiss

In the dark before dawn, I sit

Debate what sort of life this is

Betrayed the world in a single frame
the realm has all
but liquified
low I quiver
in hallowed silence
the cyst of ignorance
will time abide
ostracized
by mere fear
awaiting the lynch mob
soaked with royal sin
could differences
lead to a better truth
Nair to the gallows would I tread
but hold my head high
with clean reputation
but no
Difference is the king of dread

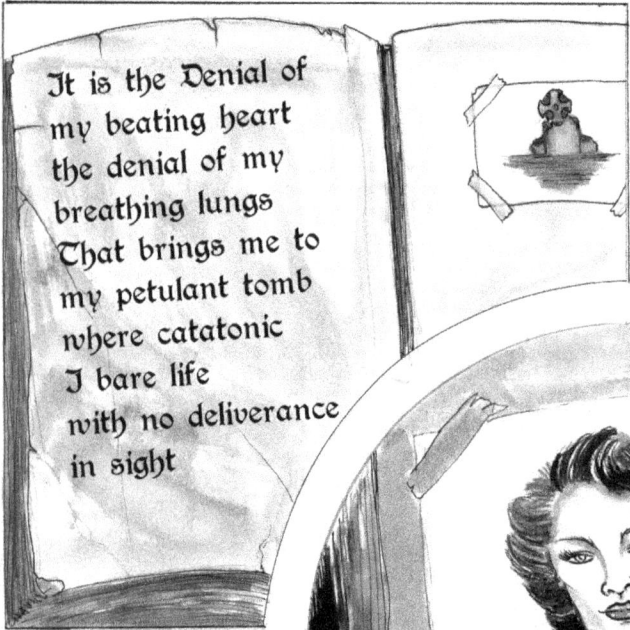

It is the Denial of
my beating heart
the denial of my
breathing lungs
That brings me to
my petulant tomb
where catatonic
I bare life
with no deliverance
in sight

Dismissed is joy and revere
And blinded by the truth
In one town the
apocalypse came
and shook the
foundation to
the ground

All began for
What I wanted most
Wasn't mine to take
But how could I refuse such lips
And ever such a fragrant kiss

In the dark before
dawn I sit
Debate what
sort of life
this is

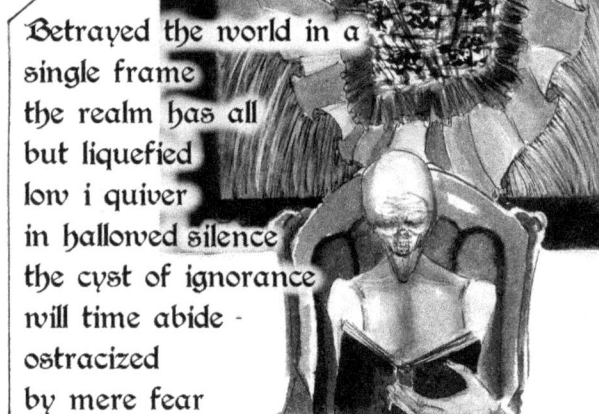

Betrayed the world in a
single frame
the realm has all
but liquefied
low i quiver
in hallowed silence
the cyst of ignorance
will time abide -
ostracized
by mere fear

awaiting the lynch mob
soaked with royal sin
could differences
lead to a better truth
Nair to the gallows would i tread
but hold my head high
with clean reputation
but no
Difference is the king of dread

Her Lips Were Green With Envy

He wasn't afraid of her
It was her lips
That made him tremble
With fright
For they were green with envy
Over the love he felt for his girl

I'd Just Like To Say

I'd just like to say
Fuck You
But when I do
You curl me up in a ball
And toss me around the room

Nothing Personal

I want you dead
But it's nothing personal
Just can't stand to see you
Without hands around your neck

I want you dead

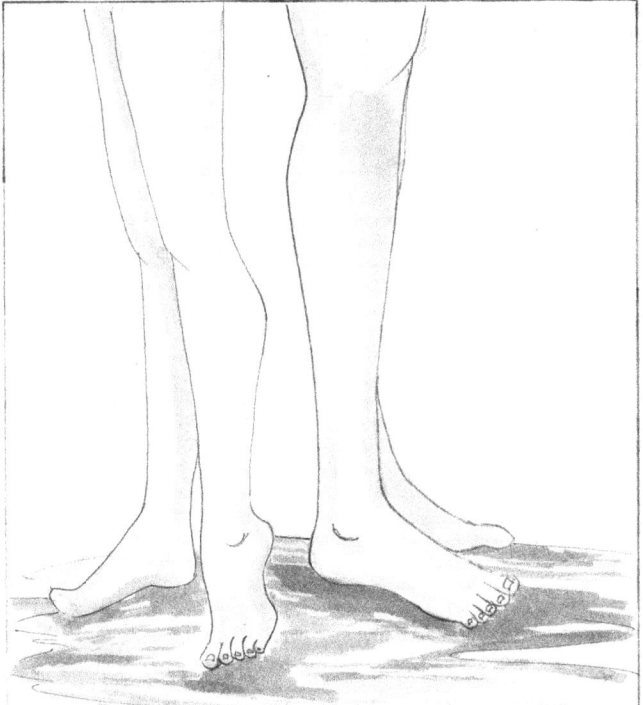

But it's nothing personal

Just can't stand to see you

Without hands around your neck

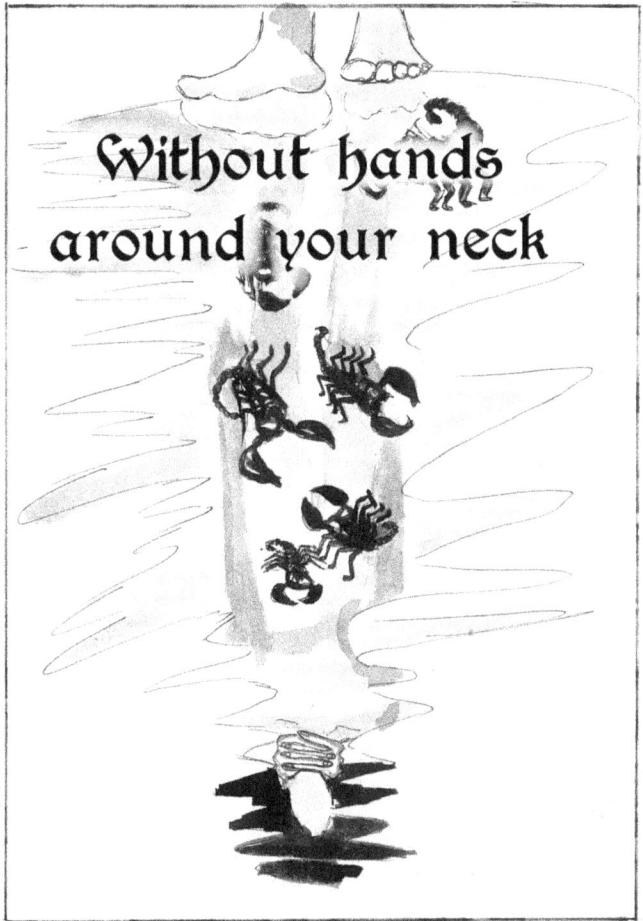

Love Is Death Personified

I'm heartbroken
Choking on the lies
I'm a soul so lost and beaten
I don't know if I can survive
Good for awhile
Then comes my denial
As they smile
Cuz they've got me fooled
Fall apart, break my heart
You never see the blames on you
I am broken, crying, lost but trying
To stand on my own
I keep falling, bleeding, screaming, weeping
As I go

Second chances just mean
You get to break me twice
Chastised by others for being too nice
Holding on so tightly to past memories
Cuz memories are all I have
People change and throw you away
And even good people will walk all over you
To get what they need
I know one thing is true
Good people are hard to find
And love is like a noose
Squeezes tighter
Throat on fire
Love will kill me
Love is death personified

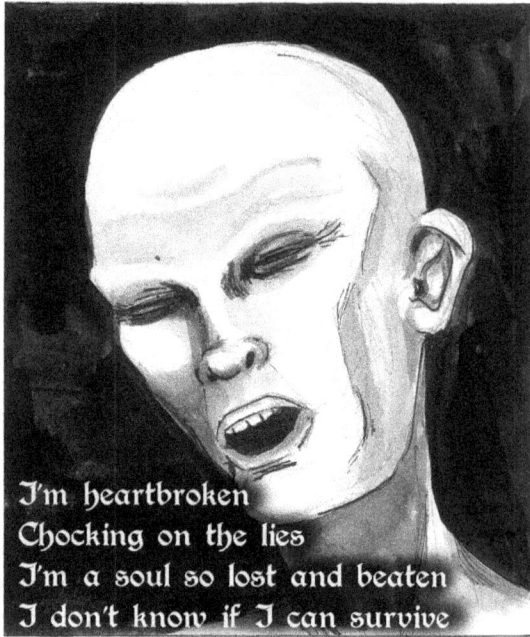

I'm heartbroken
Chocking on the lies
I'm a soul so lost and beaten
I don't know if I can survive

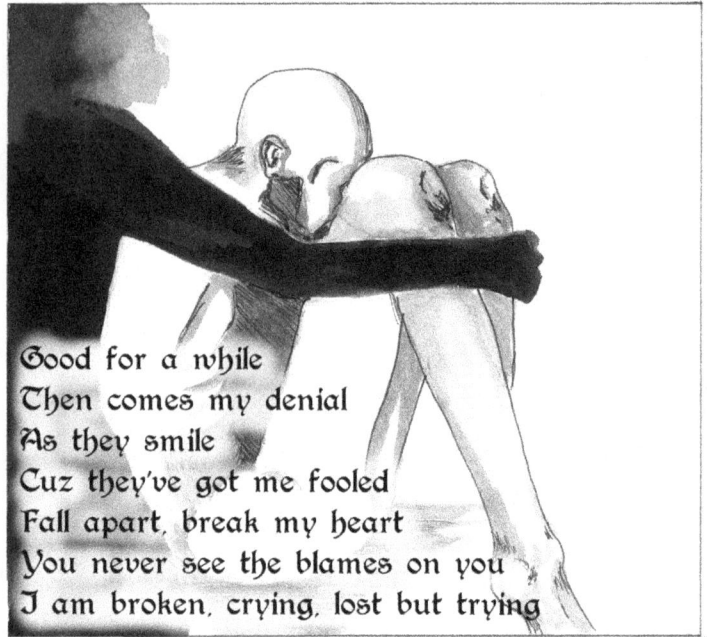

Good for a while
Then comes my denial
As they smile
Cuz they've got me fooled
Fall apart, break my heart
You never see the blames on you
I am broken, crying, lost but trying

To stand on my own
I keep falling, bleeding,
screaming, weeping
As I go

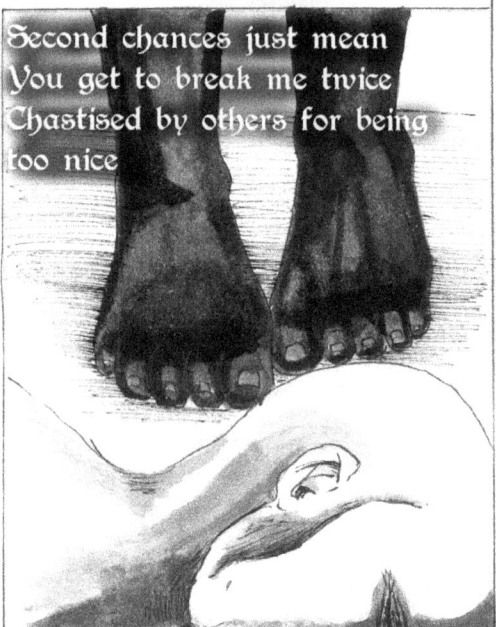

Second chances just mean
You get to break me twice
Chastised by others for being
too nice

Holding on so tightly to past
memories
Cuz memories are all I have
People change and throw you away
And even good people will walk all
over you
To get what they need
I know one thing is true
Good people are hard to find
And love is like a noose
Squeezes tighter
Throat on fire
Love will kill me
Love is death personified

Dying

Dying doesn't make you perfect
It just makes you gone

Turn Away From Grace

Turn away from grace
Make one mistake
I beg of you
Perfection in its simplicities
Is not all it's cracked up to be

Darkest Inferno

The darkest inferno

One ever faced

A touch from the reaper's scythe

Down I fall into everlasting ice

Whom lacerates, burns, mutilates, and despairs

Hearts reach out to the fire

Being burnt is their desire

For no soul holds a candle to the flame

No God reaches down to save

A heart so singed by sin

The dark inferno

Manifests

Into a man in his Sunday best

The horror of his etherial laugh

Cannot be matched by earthly chorus

And pray that we may be saved

Lucifer licks his lips with acid tongue

For I am the prey and he the hunter

He reaches out with flaming hand

A scream does part between my lips

I awaken in my bed

Shivering in a cold sweat

The dark inferno but a dream

The Darkest inferno
One ever faced
A touch from the reaper's scythe
Down I fall into everlasting ice
Whom lacerates, burns, mutilates, and despairs

Hearts reach out to the fire
Being burnt is their desire

For no soul holds a candle to the flame
No God reaches down to save
A heart so singed by sin
The dark inferno
Manifests
Into a man in his Sunday best
The horror of his ethereal laugh
Cannot be matched by earthly chorus
And pray that we may be saved

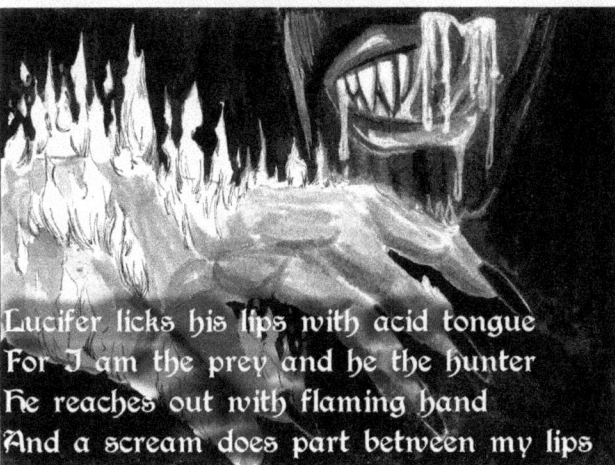

Lucifer licks his lips with acid tongue
For I am the prey and he the hunter
He reaches out with flaming hand
And a scream does part between my lips

I awaken in my bed
Shivering in a cold sweat
The dark inferno but a dream

Logically Crazy

You fell in love

With an optical illusion

All you have

A memory of the time

When you should have walked away

So now you're

Dancing on hot acid

And the bullets flying at you

Are the answers to the questions

You won't ask

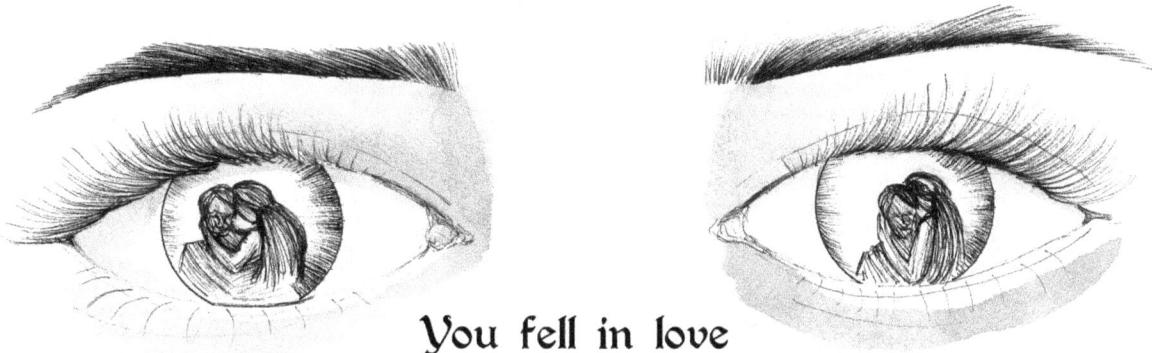

You fell in love
With an optical illusion

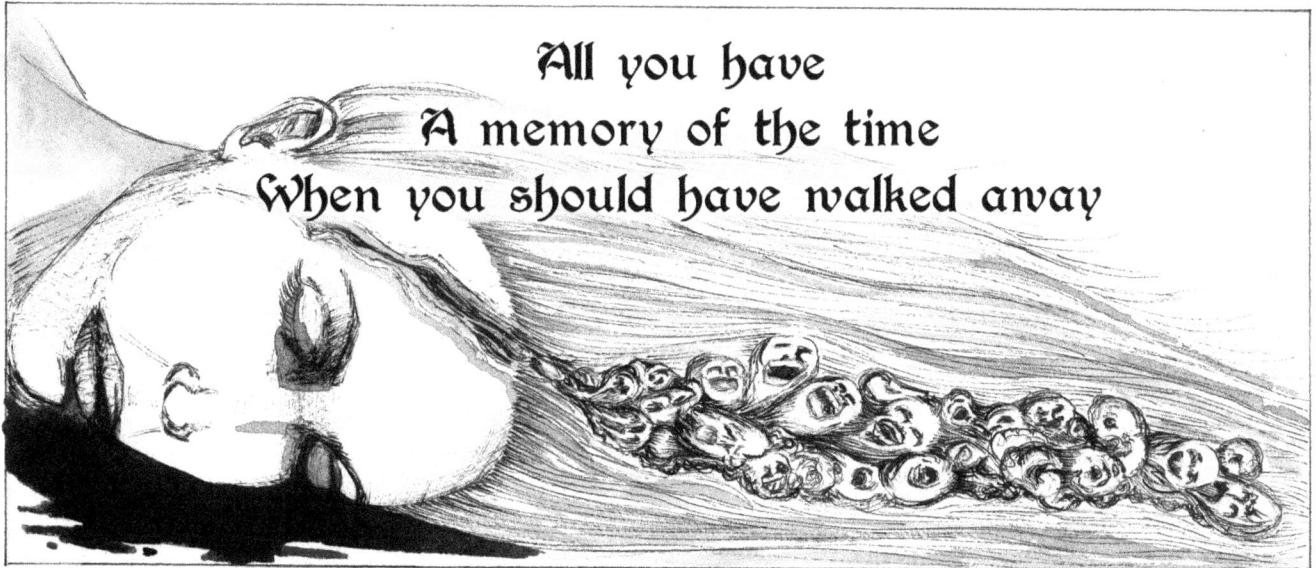

All you have
A memory of the time
When you should have walked away

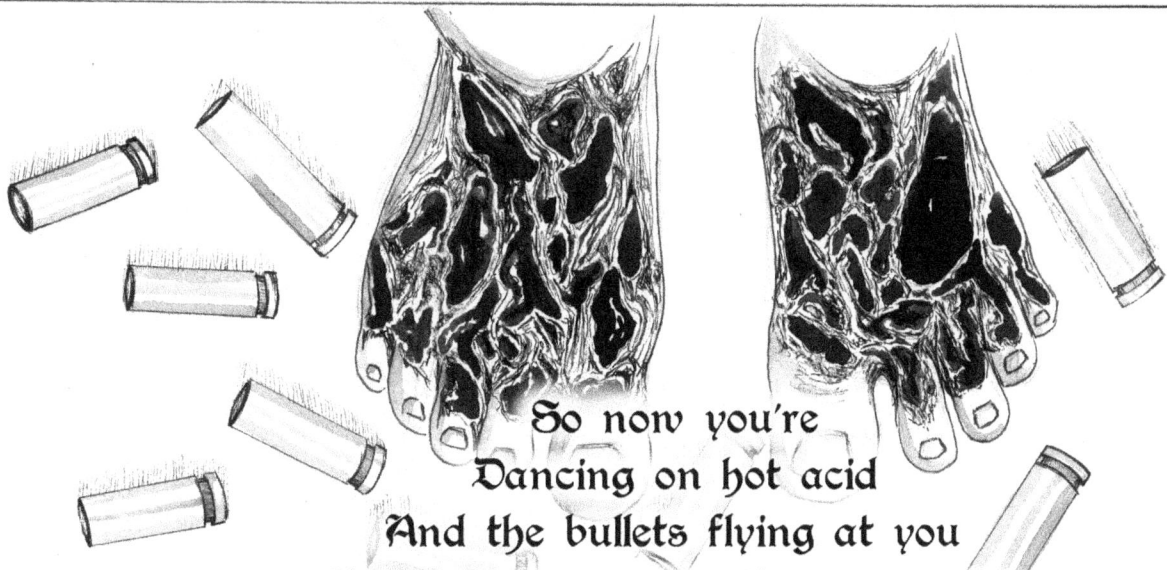

So now you're
Dancing on hot acid
And the bullets flying at you
Are the answers to the questions
You won't ask

Scarlet Wyvern

The Ghost Of Janet

When we were young

I extended my hand

Waiting and Patient

Wanting to understand

To trust took you time

But eventually you saw my pure intentions

The love in my soul

I never once left your side

Even when you pushed me away

And when something

Cracked

In your mind

I lied to myself

because I wanted you to stay

My hand was always there but now

 you grip it tight

In a strange sadistic

desperate vice

Who you are

68

and who you were
Are in no way the same
She was damaged
You're insane
My love for who you used to be
is infinite but
for who you've become
so possessive of me
I'm trying to pull my hand away
As you torment me
Stay,stay,stay

I've lost you
You're gone
You crushed my heart
So let me go
Think what you want
But
You can't love me if
You simply can't love

Your heart's been destroyed
Your soul faded away
Don't say you're here to stay
I once said id never walk away
But the girl I said that to is dead
You took her place
 The cracks in your sanity
Reflected in my heart
When you shattered
My soul tore apart

Those jade eyes
a storm at sea
the pain you hid away
A child should know love
But when you were hurt
They looked away
How could you know
how to trust
How could I expect you to stay sane
When the only comfort you had as a child
Was cocaine
I miss you
And my soul is sewn back together
But the piece that was yours
Will never mend

When we were young
I extended my hand
Waiting and Patient
Wanting to understand
To trust took you
time
But eventually,
you saw my
pure intentions
The love
in my
soul

I never once left your side
Even when you pushed
away
And when something
Cracked
In your mind
I lied to myself

because I wanted you to stay
My hand was always there
but now
you grip it tight
In a strange sadistic
desperate vice
Who you are
and who you
were

Are in no way the same
She was damaged
You're insane
My love for who you used
to be
is infinite but
for who you've become
so possessive of me
I'm trying to pull my hand
away
As you torment me
Stay, stay, stay

I've lost you
You're gone
You crushed my heart
So let me go
Think what you want
But
You can't love me if
You simply can't love
Your hearts been destroyed
Your soul faded away
Don't say you're here to stay
I once said I'd never walk
away

But the girl I said that
to is dead
You took her place
The cracks in your
sanity
Reflected in my heart
When you shattered
My soul tore apart
Those jade eyes
a storm at sea
the pain you hid away
A child should know love
But when you were hurt
They looked away
How could you know
how to trust

How could I expect you to
stay sane
When the only comfort
you had as a child
Was cocaine
I miss you
And my soul is sewn back
together
But that piece that was
yours
Will never mend

71

The Beauty Of Her Decomposition

Blowflies

Laying eggs inside her ear

Her blue eyes, glossy

No one knows how much I fear

She's decomposing on the lawn

So lovely in the dawn light

A cop walking by

Stops

"She's a lovely sight" he ponders

Then cups my breast as if to say hello

And off into oblivion, he walks

I strip myself of all my clothes

Naked, walk across the lawn

As all the neighbors gawk

I lay myself down beside her

And snuggle against her rotting flesh

Picking maggots from her eyes

Laying them upon my chest

I kiss her and taste the decay

The insects crawling up my tongue

I pull away and retch

Then lay my head back down again

Two women laying on the ground

Naked but for our skin

One is decomposing, slowly renewing

One is breaking, spiraling down

Trying to catch herself

Blowflies
Laying eggs inside her ear
Her blue eyes, glossy
No one knows how much I fear
She's decomposing on the lawn
So lovely in the dawn light

A cop walking by
Stops
"She's a lovely sight" he ponders
Then cups my breast as if to say hello
And off into oblivion, he walks
I strip myself of all my clothes
Naked, walk across the lawn

As all the neighbors gawk
I lay myself down beside
And snuggle against her rotting flesh
Picking maggots from her eyes

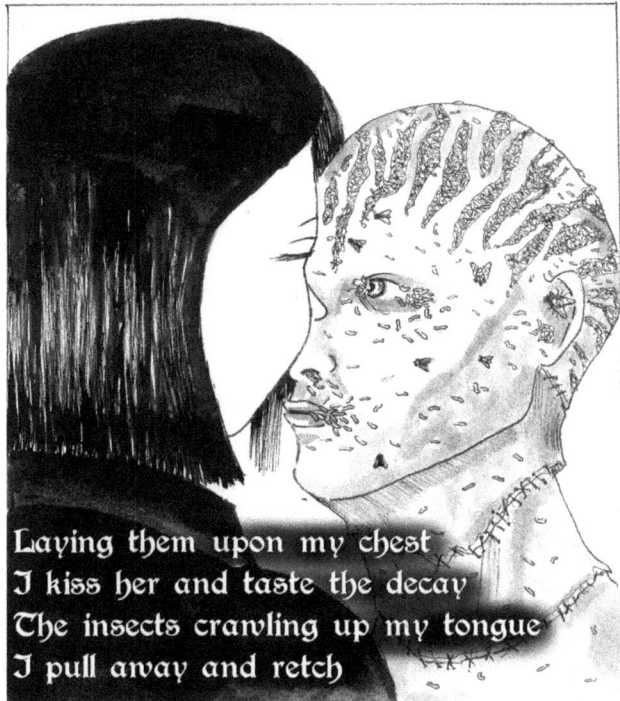

Then lay my head back
down again
Two women laying on
the ground
Naked but for our skin
One is decomposing,
slowly renewing
One is breaking,
spiraling down
Trying to catch herself

Laying them upon my chest
I kiss her and taste the decay
The insects crawling up my tongue
I pull away and retch

73

On Friendship

If I wanted to get screwed all the time
I would have become a hooker

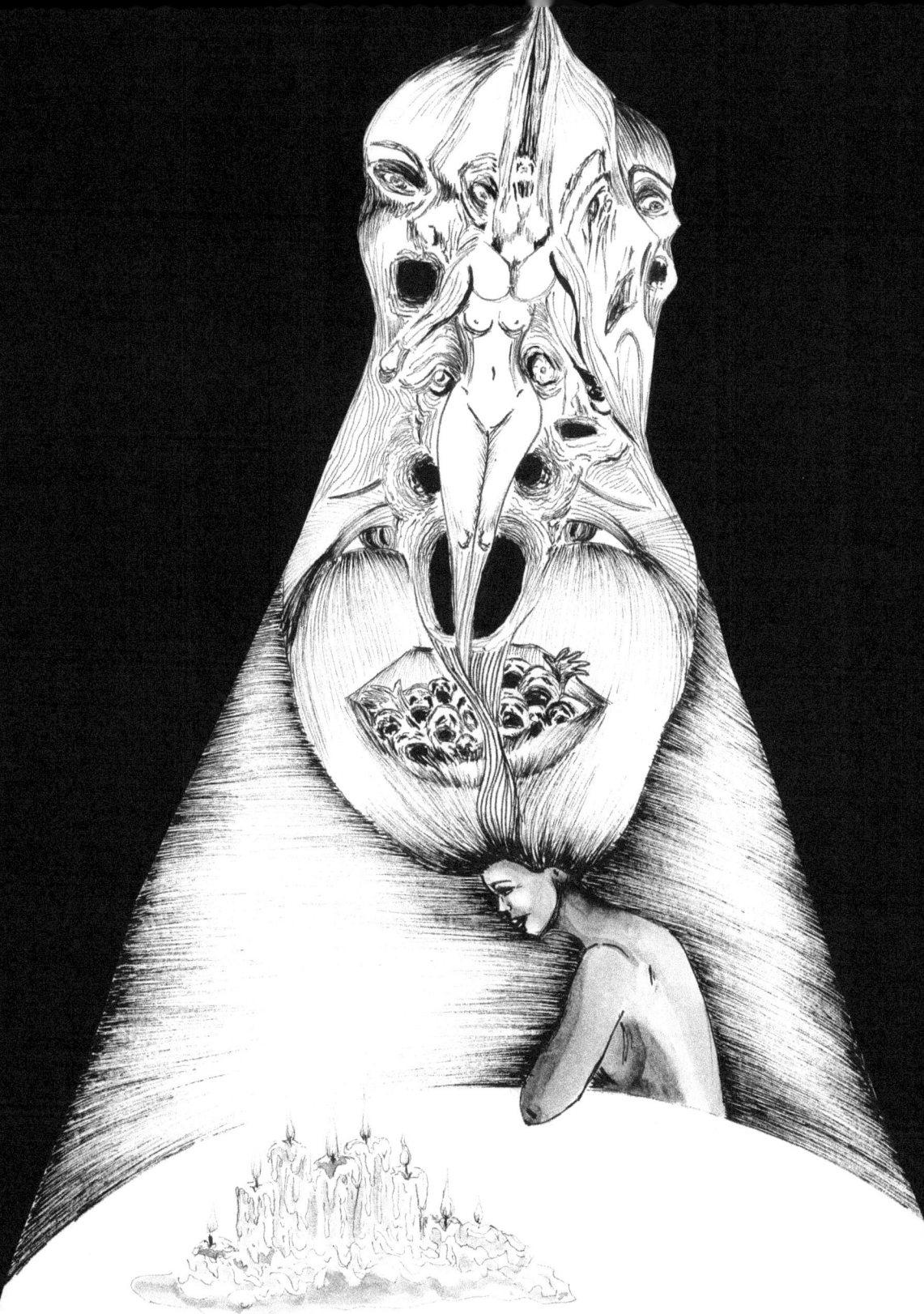

If I wanted to get screwed all the time
I would have become a hooker

I Darken

Good shan't fight
The darkness without
For then
A devilish seedling sprout
Its roots to twist and grip tight
to the soul
Blackening the purity
Subtle
Diabolically enticing to
Sultry sin
Seducing the dark sproutling within
Feed it hate
And feel it flourish in your bones
And I darken

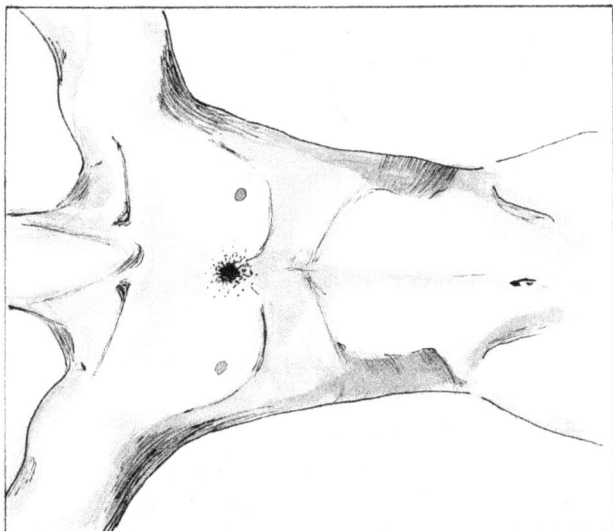

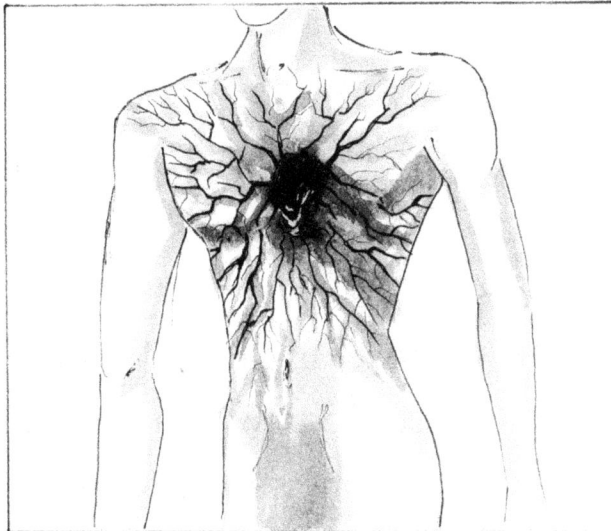

Good shan't fight
The darkness without
For then
A devilish seedling sprout
Its roots to twist and grip
tight
To the soul
Blackening the purity
Subtle

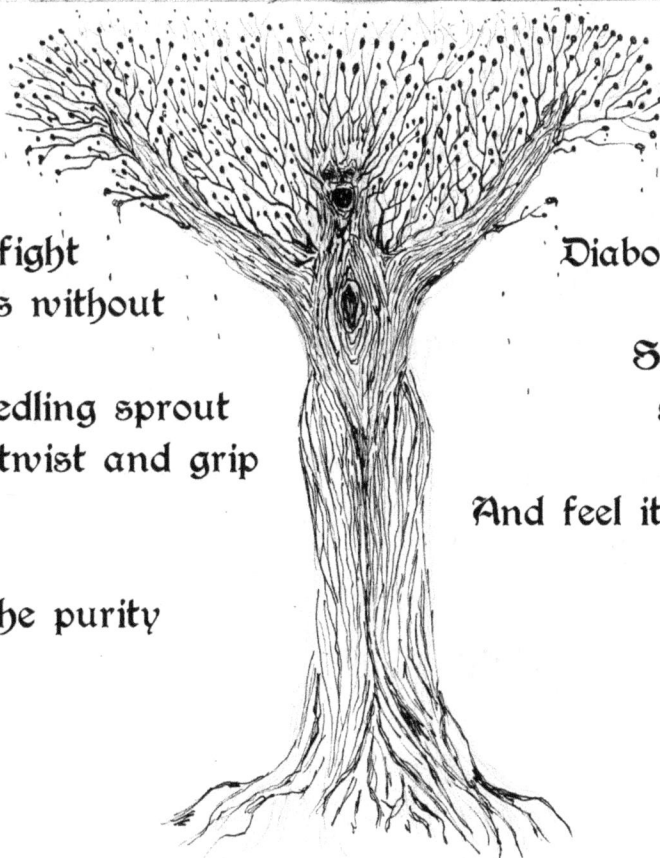

Diabolically enticing to
Sultry sin
Seducing the dark
sproutling within
Feed it hate
And feel it flourish in your
bones
And I darken

Good Little Girl

Reaching for a hand to hold that simply isn't there
Locked away and all alone
No one seems to care
Never moving forward
Only spiraling down
No one seems to notice

What else do you expect

You can't ever be yourself
Too crazy and too broken
Wishing that you couldn't feel
But your heart is too wide open
And through all the shattered pieces
You still find ways to love
It's hell to be hurt by the ones you care for
It's worse when you give up
Fought too hard
Lost too much
Broken by this world
Time to sit here quietly
And be a good little girl

Reaching for a hand to hold
that simply isn't there
Locked away and all alone
No one seems to care

Never moving forward
Only spiraling down
No one seems to notice
What else do you expect

You can't ever be yourself
Too crazy and too broken

Wishing that you couldn't feel
But your heart is too wide
open
And through all the shattered
pieces
You still find ways to love
It's hell to be hurt by the
ones you care for

It's worse when you give up
Fought too hard
Lost too much
Broken by this world
Time to sit here quietly
And be a good little girl

Dial Tone

911
Dial tone
How can I help you
I don't know
My shattered heart
Lays on the floor
The threads unravel
I am no more
My legs are numb
And I can't feel
I wish I knew
Which world is real
The sun my savior
Do not tear my mind away
A sea of lies
Reveals the truth
There's nothing left
To being you

911
Dial tone
How can I help you

I don't know
My shattered heart
Lays on the floor
The threads unravel
I am no more

My legs are numb
And I can't feel
I wish I knew
Which world is real
The sun my savior
Do not betray
Do not tear my mind away

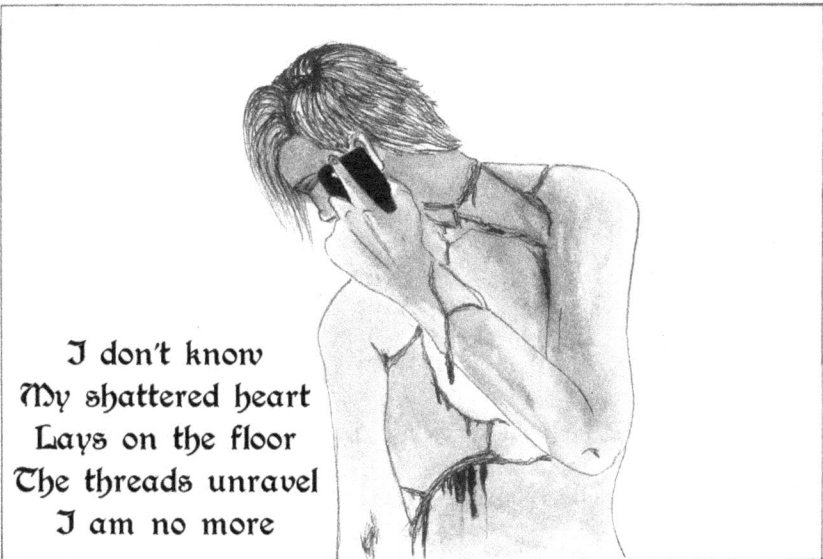

A sea of lies
Reveals the truth
There's nothing left
To being you

When She First Told Me

It's not as if I didn't long suspect
It was in the way she held herself
The mask she built from scratch
They never saw passed
But to me, it looked like glass stained
Underneath she was so beautiful and pained
I saw the tears that never slid down her face
And the fear she held inside
The distrust of anyone too kind
It took years to win her trust
I cared too much to give up

But when she first told me
Looking scared and lonely
Trying not to show it
Cheeks flushing when she met my eyes
Twisted hatred filled my lungs
My heart slowed its beating
Trying to keep a calm expression
Listening to every horrid word
Wishing I could go back in time
Stop those men from touching her

Taking the innocence of a child
Family members in denial
Horrified
What I suspected was true
So happy when her uncle died
Now I knew the reason why
Feeling a darkness swell inside
Hatred for the one alive
Rage for what he had done
Fear he'd hurt another one
Another child
She followed a dark path
When these monsters broke her fragile innocence
Found her way back to the light
Strong, resilient
Still haunted by
The kind of wound that doesn't heal
Always breaking
Never broken
Horrible images behind my eyes
of a trembling, scared abused little girl
I'll never forget the look in her eyes
When she first told me

It's not as if I didn't long suspect
It was in the way she held herself
The mask she built from scratch

They never saw passed
But to me it looked like glass stained

The distrust of anyone too kind
It took years to win her trust
I cared too much to give up

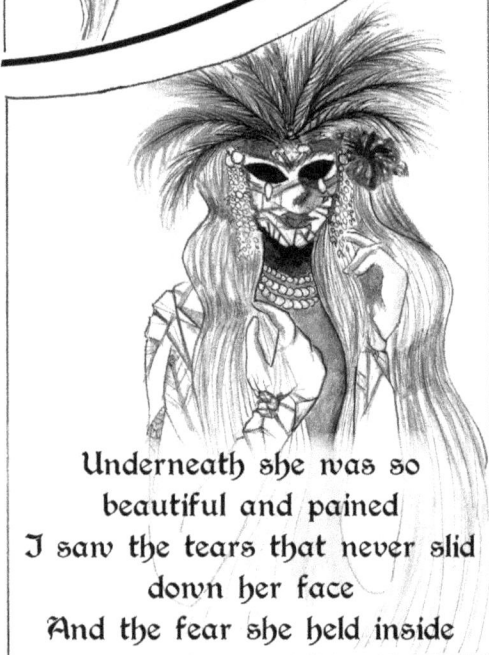

But when she first told me
Looking scared and lonely
Trying not to show it

Underneath she was so
beautiful and pained
I saw the tears that never slid
down her face
And the fear she held inside

Cheeks flushing when she met my eyes
Twisted hatred filled my lungs
My heart slowed its beating
Trying to keep a calm expression
Listening to every horrid word
Wishing I could go back in time
Stop those men from touching her
Taking the innocence of a child
Family members in denial
Horrified
What I suspected was true
So happy when her uncle died
Now I knew the reason why
Feeling a darkness swell inside
Hatred for the one alive
Rage for what he had done

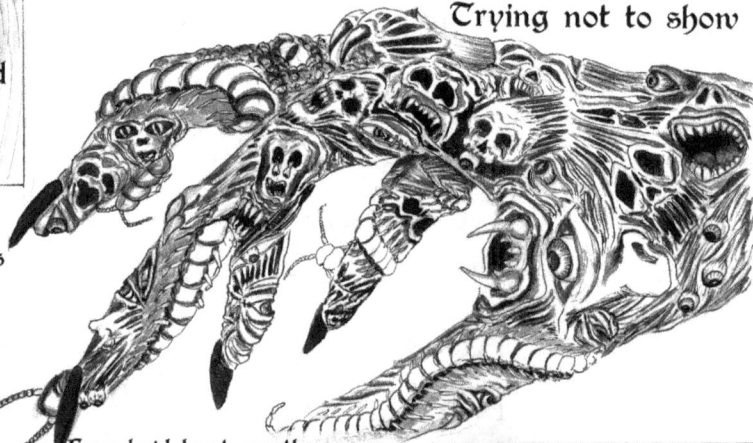

Fear he'd hurt another one
Another child
She followed a dark path
When these monsters broke her
fragile innocence
Found her way back to the light
Strong, resilient
Still haunted by
The kind of wound that
doesn't heal
Always breaking
Never broken

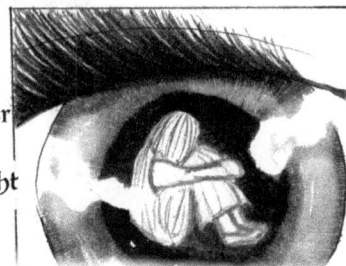

Horrible images behind my eyes
of a trembling, scared abused little girl
I'll never forget the look in her eyes
When she first told me

I Bought Myself A Coffin

I bought myself a coffin
Today I lay inside
I pull the lid closed above me
And now I wait to die

If You Can Smile

If you can smile
For just a while
Maybe so can I

A Torch And A Welcome Mat

All you've got

Is a torch and a welcome mat

Burn them down

Wipe your feet

Before you head inside

Set fire to the lies

Burn down the facade

All you've got

Is a sinking heart

Soaked in fire

A shattering heart

Splintered glass

Love was never meant to last

You're all I thought

You'd never be

An infected soul

And I, the carrier of your disease

All you've got
Is a torch and a welcome mat
Burn them down
Wipe your feet

Before you head inside
Set fire to the lies
Burn down the façade
All you've got
Is a sinking heart
Soaked in fire

A shattering heart
Splintered glass
Love was never meant to last
You're all I thought

You'd never be
An infected soul
And I, the carrier of your disease

The Storm

There is a storm coming

And I'm afraid

The snake entrances me

Take the apple in your hand

One bite won't hurt no one

From outside the gate I'm looking in

The snake hisses out a laugh

How easily I fall into his trap

There is a storm coming

And I am going with it

Hurled into the air

Swirling past the trees

Curled into a ball

Cut by the debris

And the storm comes

She looks at me entranced

Take the apple in your hand

One bite can't hurt

From outside the gate she's looking in

Now I am the snake

But at least now I am heard

There is a storm coming

And I'm a part of it

Hurling through the air

Cutting through the trees

Hissing on the wind

Passing the disease

There is a storm coming
And I'm afraid
The snake entrances me
Take the apple in your hand

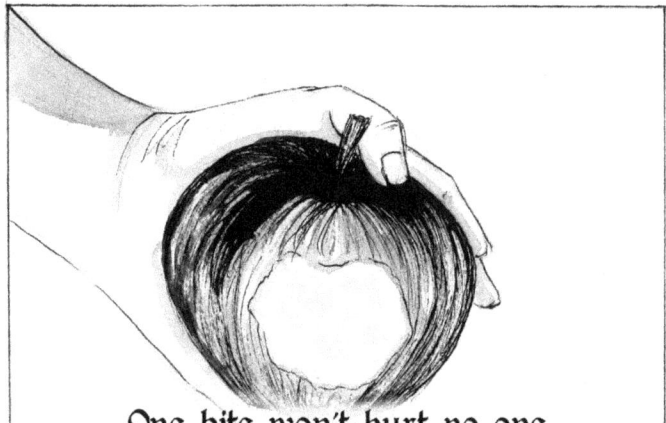

One bite won't hurt no one
From outside the gate, I'm looking in
The snake hisses out a laugh
How easily I fall into his trap

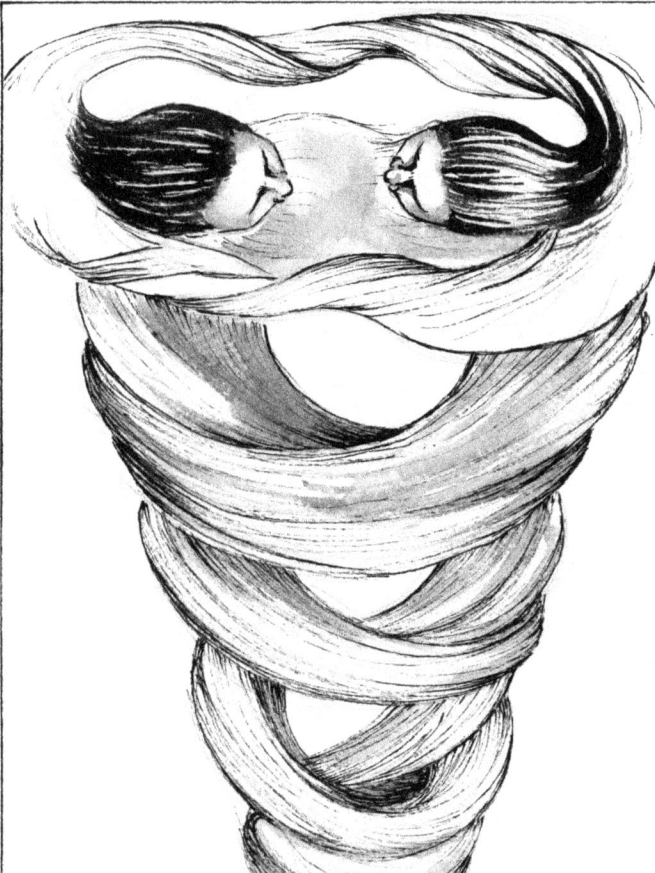

One bite can't hurt
From outside the gate, she's looking in
Now I am the snake
But at least now I am heard
There is a storm coming
And I'm a part of it

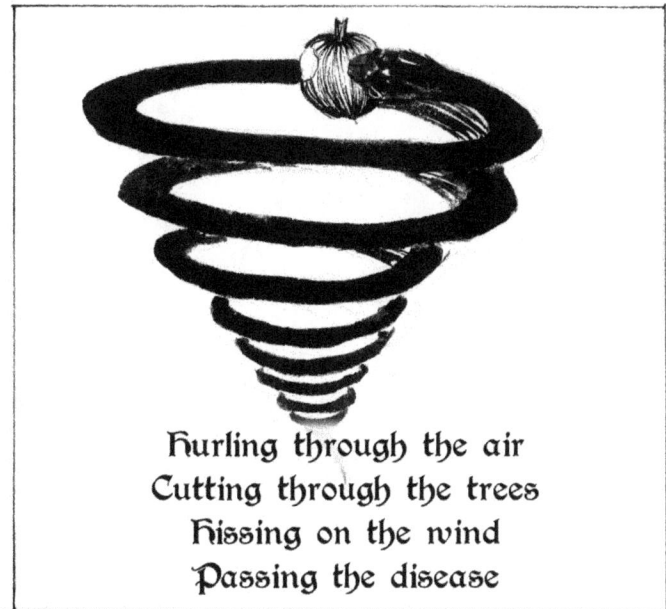

There is a storm coming
And I am going with it
Hurled into the air
Swirling past the trees
Curled into a ball
Cut by the debris
And the storm comes
She looks at me entranced
Take the apple in your hand

Hurling through the air
Cutting through the trees
Hissing on the wind
Passing the disease

89

To The Seven Seas

And everything you tell me so for ashes

I can not seem to find a way

To prove that I have sinned

When everything you say is dug beneath the grave

I never told a lie that wasn't fatal

To the seven seas

There is a saying

You get what you deserve

And everything you tell
me is for ashes
I can not seem to find
a way

To prove that I have sinned
When everything you say is dug
beneath the grave

I never told a lie that wasn't
fatal
To the seven seas
There is a saying
You get what you deserve

Against The Limit

Against the limit
I can feel the dust of you
The flutter of your eyelids against my chest
I am
The clutter on the floor that you haven't bothered to throw out
You are an arrow in my head
A porcelain drug
As you shatter
I stutter
Love engulfs and decays
You, the misdirection
Well I'm lost
But I'm looking
For the breadcrumbs
You left behind
With my new found eyes
Maybe I will find my way home
And you

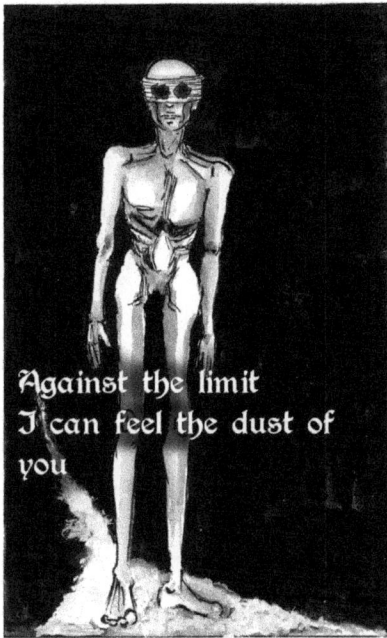

Against the limit
I can feel the dust of
you

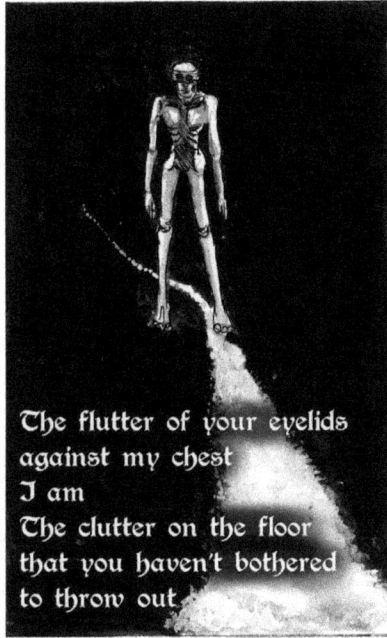

The flutter of your eyelids
against my chest
I am
The clutter on the floor
that you haven't bothered
to throw out

You are an arrow in my
head
A porcelain drug
As you shatter
I stutter

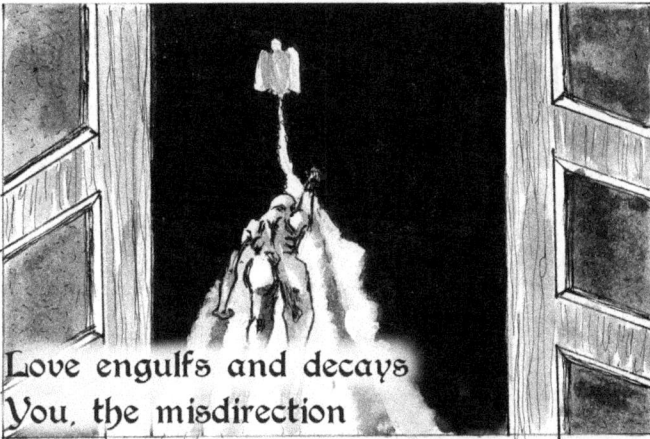

Love engulfs and decays
You, the misdirection

Well I'm lost
But I'm looking
For the breadcrumbs
You left behind

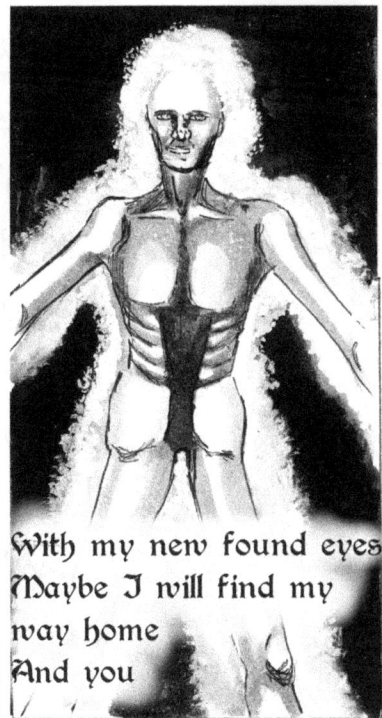

With my new found eyes
Maybe I will find my
way home
And you

93

The Dirt Under Your Skin

The dirt under your skin

Crawls through you

The stains don't fade

You can try to change

Your reputation always bites you back

In the ass

The dirt under my skin

It's heavy and It's deep

Weighing me down

Filling me in

Sins still stain

Conscience blows away

Wish I could melt away

I'm crashing up

The worlds coming down

Off its high

I think we're gonna collide

The dirt under your skin

I am the dirt under your skin

Oh what a relief

Oh what a sin

There's no way out

So why even try

Bet you didn't know that the dirt is alive

The dirt under your skin
Crawls through you
The stains don't fade
You can try to change
Your reputation always
bites you back
In the ass

The dirt under my skin
It's heavy, and It's
deep
Weighing me down
Filling me in
Sins still stain

Conscience blows away
Wish I could melt away
I'm crashing up
The worlds coming down
Off its high

I think we're gonna collide
The dirt under your skin
I am the dirt under your skin
Oh what a relief
Oh what a sin
There's no way out
So why even try
Bet you didn't know that the dirt is
alive

Myself

Is running me ragged
I'm on the edge of a cliff
I keep slipping off the edge
How many times can I grab the edge
How many times can you pull me up
I'm dying
Because I slipped me some poison
I'm trying to tell you
Who did this to me
But how can I tell you it was me
Me wants me dead
Me pleads for mercy
But me won't give mercy
You can't understand
Nobody can
And me hates them for it
But I don't

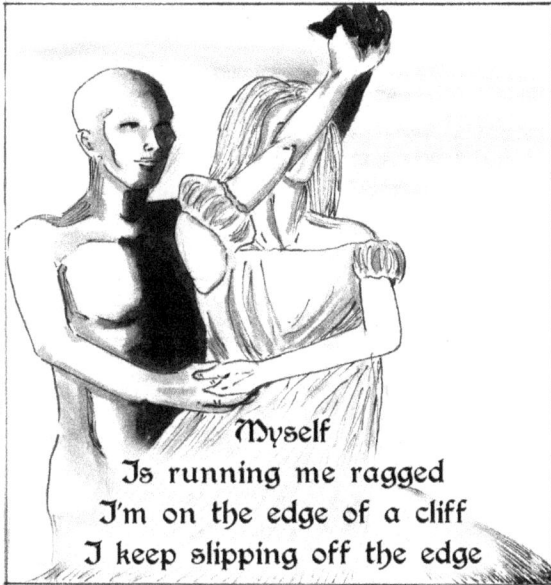

Myself
Is running me ragged
I'm on the edge of a cliff
I keep slipping off the edge

How many times can I grab the edge
How many times can you pull me up
I'm dying

Because I slipped me some poison
I'm trying to tell you
Who did this to me

But how can I tell you it was me
Me wants me dead
Me pleads for mercy

But me won't give mercy
You can't understand
Nobody can

And me hates them
for it
But I don't

Secret Of The Children

We were drowning in tears

And still they came

The one thing the rain wouldn't wash away

Was the pain in our hearts as they marched on, the rogues

And the tears in our eyes matched the ones in our souls

As they walked by I took careful aim

To see how they mocked us

And laughed at our pain

I balled up my fists and screamed in rage

My palms bled but no noise was made

We sat in the cold, injured and soaking

Surveying the dead in the silence of morning

And seeing the living we thought in our hearts

Maybe the good aren't meant for life

As we sat in the silence one thought did approach me

Annoying and fleeting and soft as it was

That perhaps I was mocking my very own pain

Perhaps I was laughing at all of us

We sat still as stone until the rain ceased its pour

With everything broken

Our home and hearts, ash

One by one we left to wander and find our own paths

The pain is still raw

Though the years have past

I am still haunted by what I couldn't undo

Only the storm carries me through

We were drowning in tears
And still they came
The one thing the rain wouldn't
wash away
Was the pain in our hearts as they
marched on, the rouges

And the tears in our eyes
matched the ones in our souls
As they walked by I took careful
aim
To see how they mocked us
And laughed at our pain

I balled up my fists and
screamed in rage
My palms bled but no noise
was made

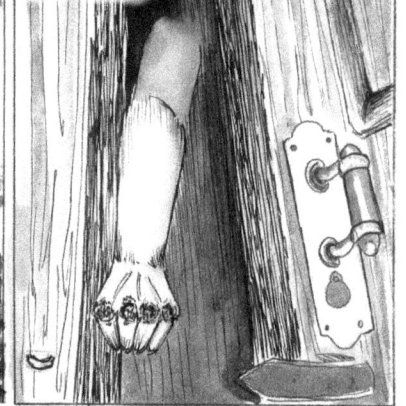

We sat in the cold, injured and soaking
Surveying the dead in the silence of morning
And seeing the living we thought in our hearts
Maybe the good aren't meant for life

As we sat in the silence one thought did approach me
Annoying and fleeting and soft as it was
That perhaps I was mocking my very own pain
Perhaps I was laughing at all of us

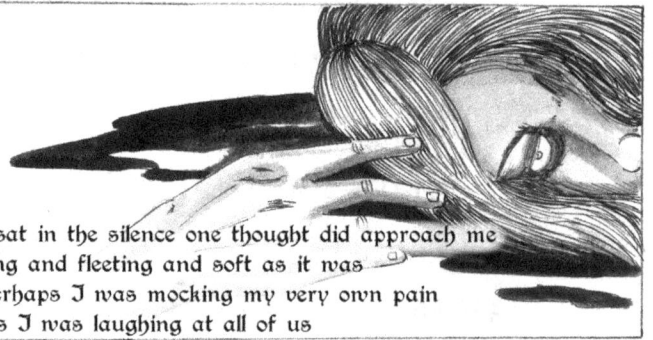

We sat still as stone until the rain ceased its pour
With everything broken
Our home and hearts, ash
One by one we left to wander and find
our own paths

The pain is still raw
Though the years have past
I am still haunted by what
I couldn't undo
Only the storm carries me
through

Dead People

Dead people are quiet
They Make good neighbors

Sin Is An Open Stage

Sin is an open stage
You walk right on
Say your lines and get paid
It's open mike night at the house of sin
It's a little risk
Well worth the tip

The Child

I'm hardly a child with my innocent eyes

I lie like a virgin

spitting venom in your eyes

Your soul is only part of you

but i rip it away

nothings meant to stay

and here

where the virgin meets her doom

spring flowers are in bloom

And with phallic smile

the virgin is with child

of err and malevolence is born

but I shall linger here

for my life is in vain

the child is my name

I'm hardly a child with my innocent eyes
I lie like a virgin

Spitting venom in your eyes
Your soul is only part of you
But I rip it away
Nothings meant to stay
And here

Where the virgin meets her doom
Spring flowers are in bloom
And with phallic smile
The virgin is with child

Of err and
malevolence is born
But I shall linger here
For my life is in vain
The child is my name

A Knife To Her Wrist

She's got a knife to her wrist

But she don't show it

Cuz the world has never loved her

And she has always known it

And if she cries for help

she knows just how it's seen

As she sobs

they say, drama queen

So she hides it deep inside

Don't expose it

And hates herself all the more

For the wrist she couldn't slit open

The knife in her nightstand

Is disappointed in her now

And her only companions are sad songs

That reflect her pain

She's got a knife to her wrist

She doesn't want it to show

She tries to smile and lie awhile

But still she hopes you know

She wants to be saved
But she can't take the pain
She is slipping down below
She's got a knife to her wrist
And you know it
But you aren't strong enough to reach out
and hold her
So you wave goodbye
You won't look her in the eye
You're bolting
She screams in pain
and slices straight
The blood bubbles up
Liquid relief
She slips down
lying on the floor
Shallow breaths and loneliness
And they find her there
A shame they say
She had a knife to her wrist
And you looked away

She's got a knife to her wrist
But she don't show it
Cuz the world has never loved her
And she has always known it
And if she cries for help
She knows just how it's seen
As she sobs
they say, drama queen

So she hides it deep inside
Don't expose it

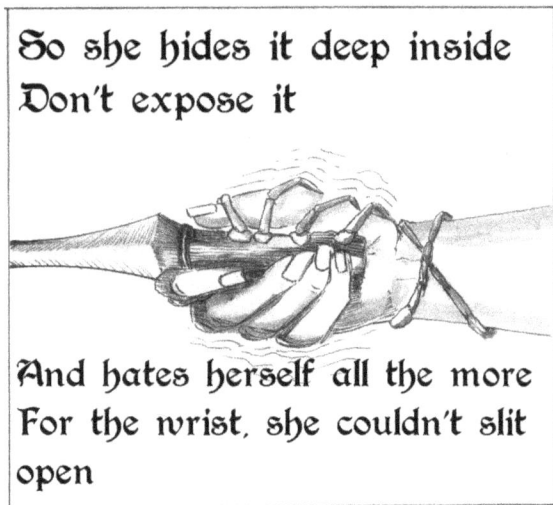

And hates herself all the more
For the wrist, she couldn't slit
open

But she can't take the pain
She is slipping down below
She's got a knife to her wrist
And you know it
But you aren't strong enough to reach out
And hold her
So you wave goodbye
You won't look her in the eye
You're bolting
She screams in pain
And slices straight
The blood bubbles up
Liquid relief
She slips down
lying on the floor
Shallow breaths and loneliness
And they find her there
A shame they say
She had a knife to her wrist
And you looked away

The knife in her nightstand
Is disappointed in her now
And her only companions are
sad songs
That reflect her pain

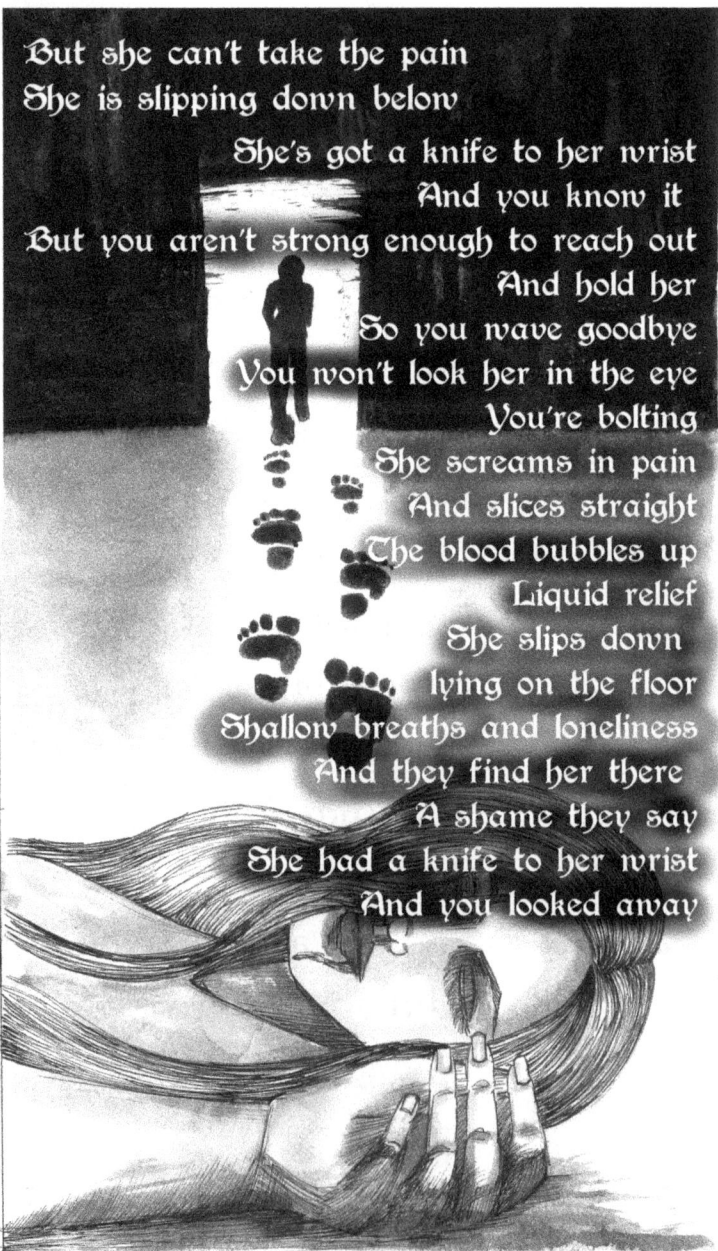

She's got a knife to her wrist
She doesn't want it to show
She tries to smile and lie awhile
But still, she hopes you know
She wants to be saved

The Vampire's Promise

In the dark, we wait
You bait us with your flushing cheeks
We sedate you with our lust

I Pretend To Hate You

I pretend to hate you
The way you hate me
Because if I didn't
I'd have to admit I still love you
And that hurts too much

My Cocoon

My cocoon is made of thorns
As I begin to grow
The thorns dig deeper into my flesh
The blood pours from my thighs and chest
I ache where the thorns reside inside me
I cannot wait for the day
I break through these walls
But the day I break out of my prison
Is the day
I die

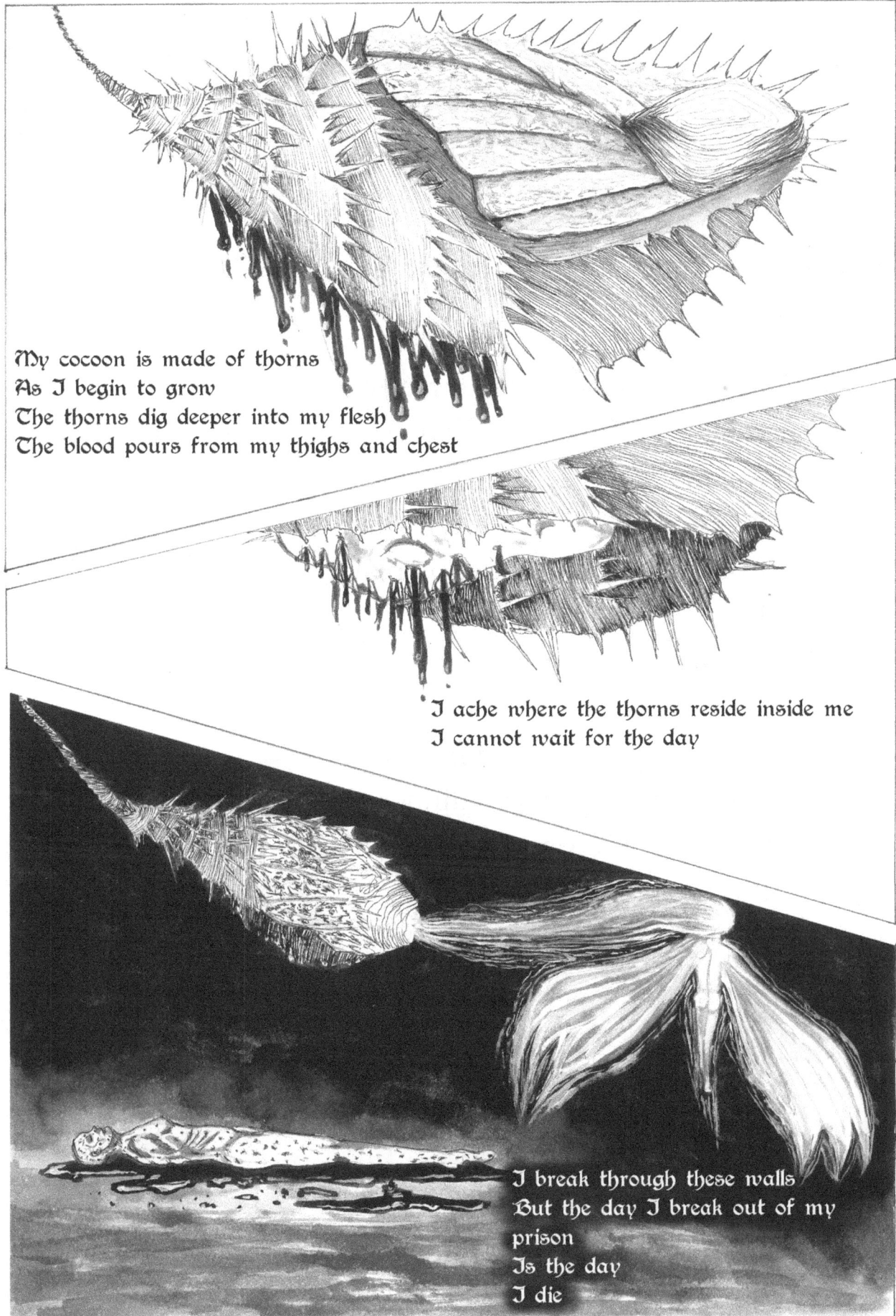

My cocoon is made of thorns
As I begin to grow
The thorns dig deeper into my flesh
The blood pours from my thighs and chest

I ache where the thorns reside inside me
I cannot wait for the day

I break through these walls
But the day I break out of my
prison
Is the day
I die

Imploding Lungs

Kill me now you fucking bastard

Kill me now, so I don't have to hang the noose

Kill me now you know you want to

Break my bones and show me truth

Just like her, you want to break me

Just like her, you hate me broken

Tighten around my neck

your hands

break the heart and suffocate

Imploding lungs on a dinner plate

I'm too broken, and you're too late

Suicide by pure heartache

Kill me now you fucking bastard
Kill me now, so I don't have to hang the
noose
Kill me now you know you want to
Break my bones and show me truth

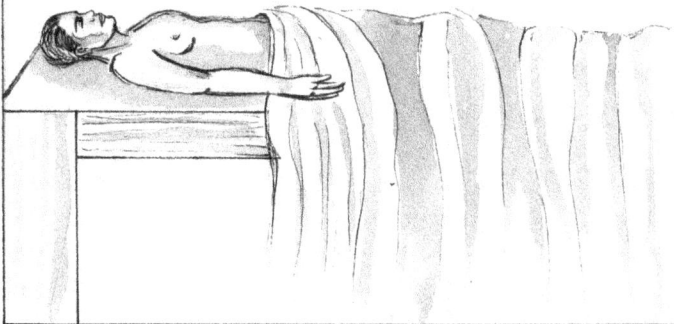

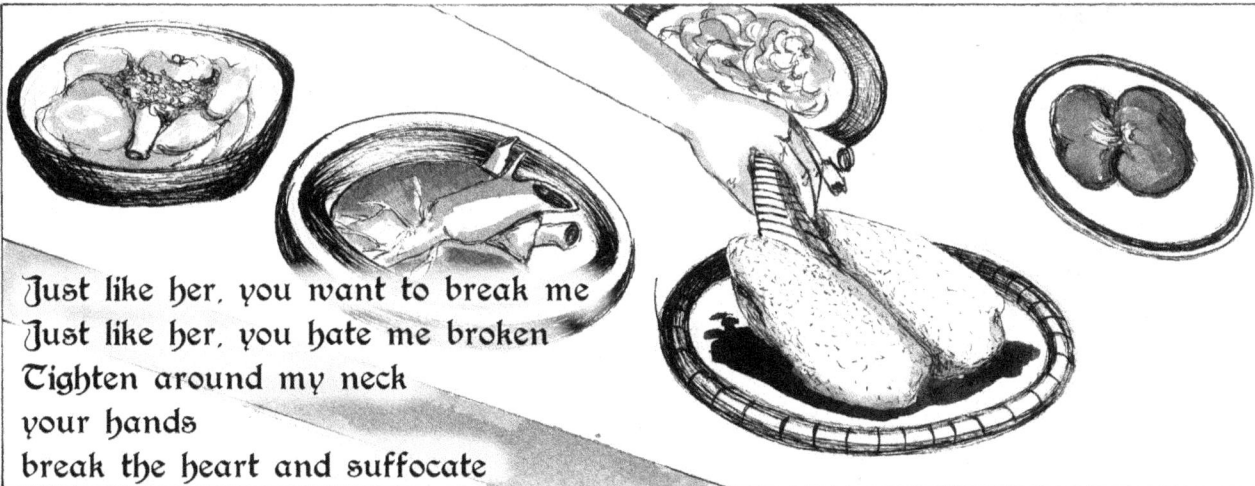

Just like her, you want to break me
Just like her, you hate me broken
Tighten around my neck
your hands
break the heart and suffocate

Imploding lungs on a dinner plate
I'm too broken, and you're too late
Suicide by pure heartache

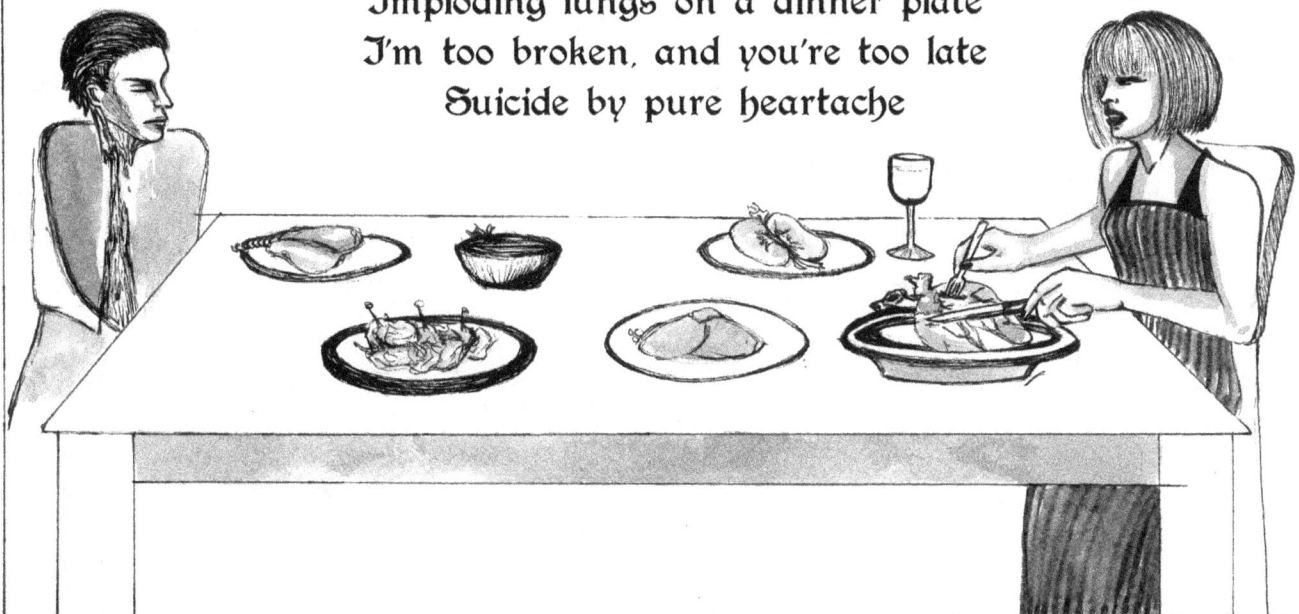

Wrath

May the fires that
Envelope you be as the fires of hell
That they may carry you downward
To reside
In the cold
Barren waste of their father's realm
And may the beast
once known
as Morning Star, himself
bare down upon your soul
A litany of torture that only the damned can inflict
For they have no souls to teach them mercy
And may you as well
torture your own soul
in seeing what you have become
And may you forever know
the meaning of eternal damnation
And may none weep over your passing
Or pray for your soul

May the fires that
Envelope you be as the fires of hell

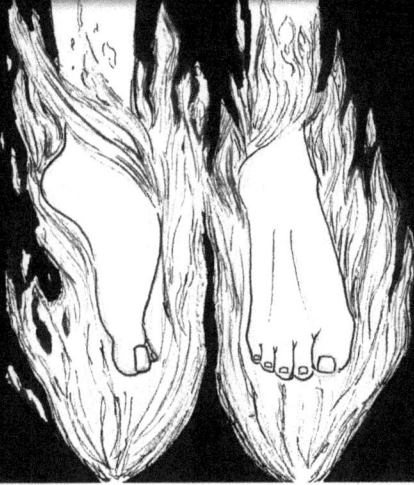

That they may carry you downward
To reside
In the cold

Barren waste of their father's realm
And may the beast
once known
as Morning Star, himself
bare down upon your soul
A litany of torture that only the damned can
inflict

For they have no souls to teach
them mercy
And may you as well
torture your own soul
in seeing
what you have become

And may you forever know
the meaning of eternal
damnation
And may none weep over
your passing
Or pray for your soul

113

The Old Man

The old man embraces me in his branches

The tree is old

A rotting corpse

Of a once vibrant sprite

I climb the arms of the trunk

Swimming in free thought

As the calming old man embraces me in his branches

One day I will come to climb

And find him on his side

A heart attack in his sleep

But for now I climb

Freeing myself from worry

A sanctuary of solitude

The old man embraces me in his branches
The tree is old
A rotting corpse

Of a once vibrant sprite
I climb the arms of the trunk
Swimming in free thought
As the calming old man embraces me in
his branches

One day I will come to climb
And find him on his side
A heart attack in his sleep

But for now, I climb
Freeing myself from worry
A sanctuary of solitude

115

She/Her

Her skin falls away in rags
It dangles from her outstretched arms
Like stalagmites in the growing dawn
I see her bow her oozing head
And pray that she is just a dream
Her eyes are blue but stained with blood
She does not see me across the plane
Of thought and sight I travel to see
Her feet twist in and her body shakes
Shimmering as she does
She disappears from all known worlds
I call out but she cannot hear
For where she stood I clearly see
She left her ribcage on the ground
I reach through the mist to grab it
But I am lost

Her skin falls away in rags
It dangles from her outstretched arms
Like stalagmites in the growing dawn

I see her bow her oozing head
And pray that she is just a dream

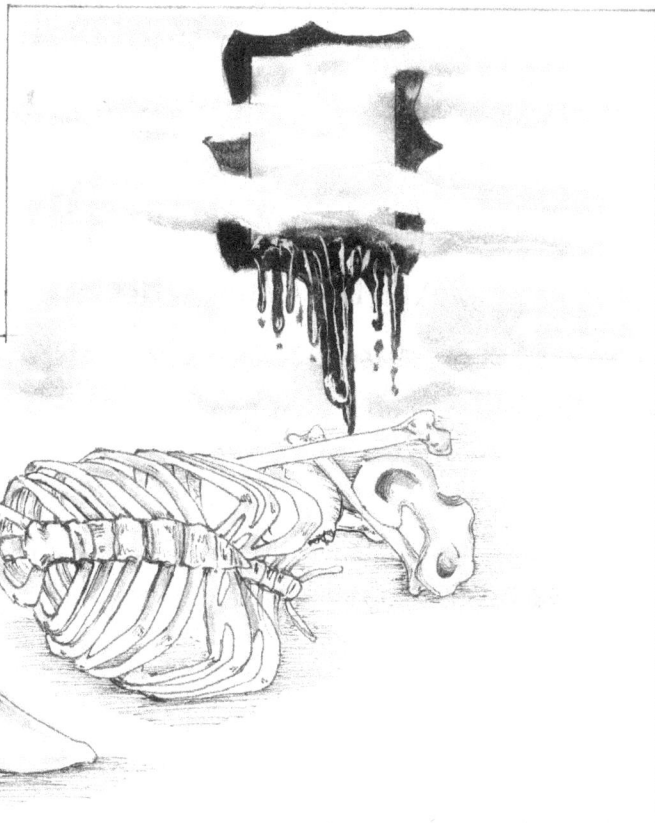

Her eyes are blue but stained with blood
She does not see me across the plane

Of thought and sight, I travel to see
Her feet twist in, and her body shakes
Shimmering as she does
She disappears from all known worlds
I call out, but she cannot hear
For where she stood I clearly see
She left her ribcage on the ground
I reach through the mist to grab it
But I am lost

Losing Too Much

Everything is shattered
Everything inside
Those you loved the most
Are the ones who lied
Love is like a poison
A knife aimed at your back
And when it pierces your heart
Your very soul will crack
Love is just deception
Trust is but a lie
And when you see the truth in this
All good in you will die
Love is an illusion
Friendship is for fools
Those who hold darkest of hearts
Are the ones who rule
There is no redemption
And love is but one way
And for all the sins within the world
The good of heart will pay

Everything is shattered
Everything inside
Those you loved
the most
Are the ones who lied

Love is like a poison
A knife aimed at your
back
And when it pierces
your heart
Your very soul will
crack

Love is just deception
Trust is but a lie
And when you see the truth in this
All good in you will die

Love is an illusion
Friendship is for fools
Those who hold darkest of hearts
Are the ones who rule

There is no redemption
And love is but one way
And for all the sins within
the world
The good of heart will pay

119

A Plea To Death

And here I am yet once more
The bearer of maddening sorrow
So tell me
Be ye of God's glory
Or devil's dark descent
How many times more will you cross my threshold
Stealing breath from those I adore
Until the bell is rung
And you come
Summoning
Summoning me to your ghastly shore

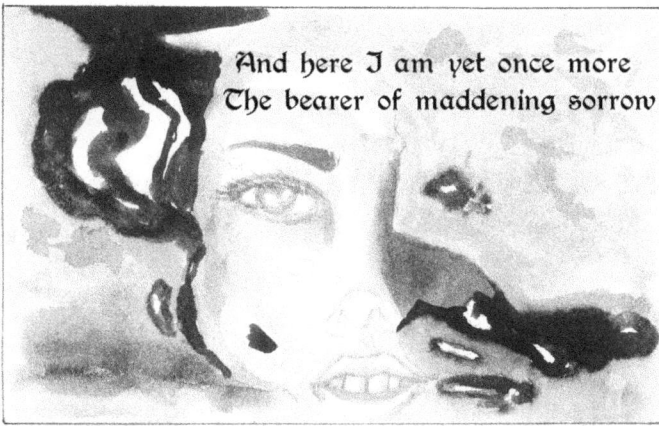

And here I am yet once more
The bearer of maddening sorrow

So tell me
Be ye of God's glory
Or devil's dark descent

How many times more will you cross my threshold
Stealing breath from those I adore

Until the bell is rung
And you come

Summoning
Summoning me to
your ghastly shore

The Monster Called Suicide

You face the monster in the mirror
He can instill no fear in you
Simultaneously you both attack
The fatal boom
No turning back
The spinning of the room
Did you win
Or did you lose
Simplicity is a luxury
One that you don't have
And as you lye bleeding to death
The monster is finally laid to rest

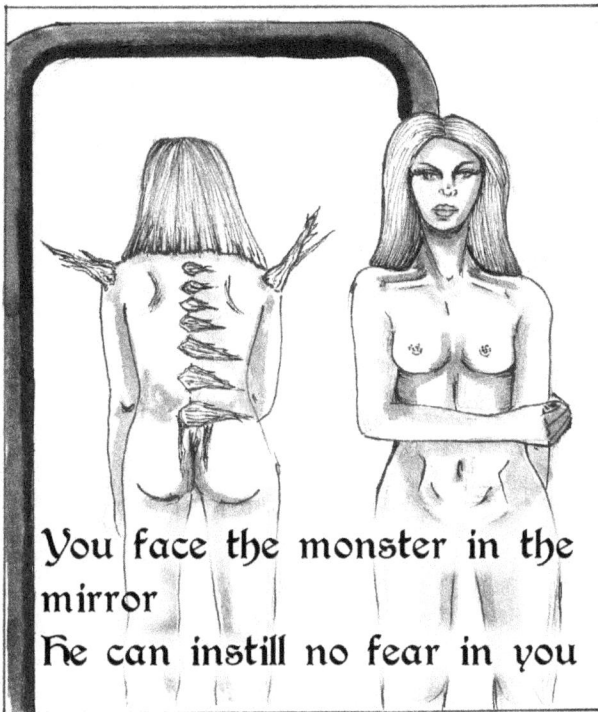

You face the monster in the mirror
He can instill no fear in you

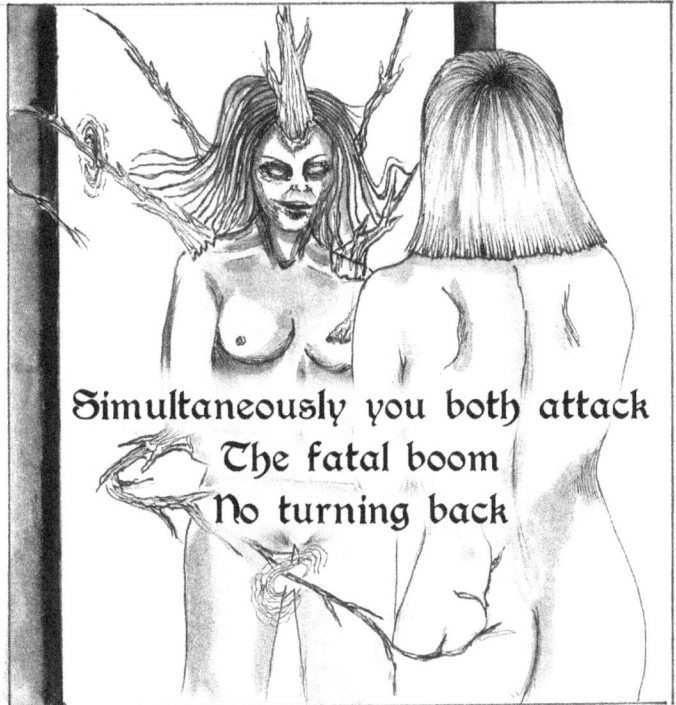

Simultaneously you both attack
The fatal boom
No turning back

The spinning of the room
Did you win
Or did you lose

Simplicity is a luxury
One that you don't have

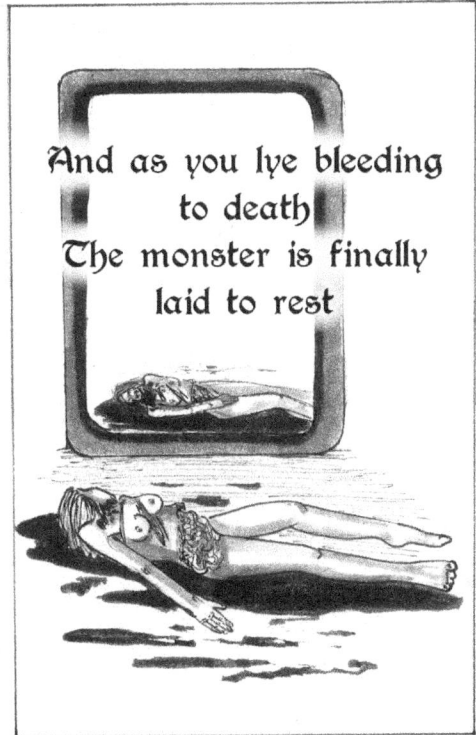

And as you lye bleeding
to death
The monster is finally
laid to rest

You And I Meet In The Water

You and I meet in the water
Face to face for the slaughter
Child of Adam
Son or daughter
We are sinners for the slaughter

We are sinners for the slaughter
Slaughter of the son and daughter
Child of Eve
Fighting harder
All avert their eyes in horror
As you and I meet in the water

You and I meet in the
water
Face to face for the
slaughter

Child of Adam
Son or daughter
We are sinners for the
slaughter

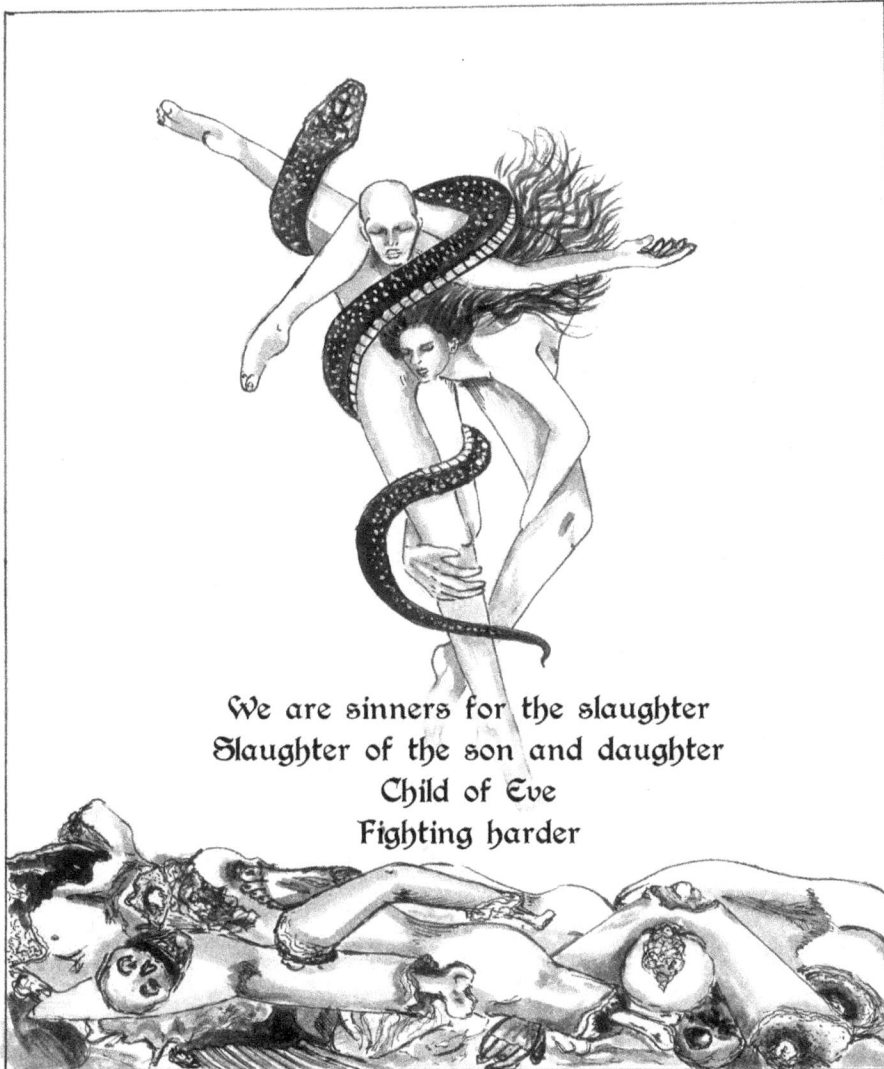

All avert their eyes in
horror
As you and I meet in
the water

We are sinners for the slaughter
Slaughter of the son and daughter
Child of Eve
Fighting harder

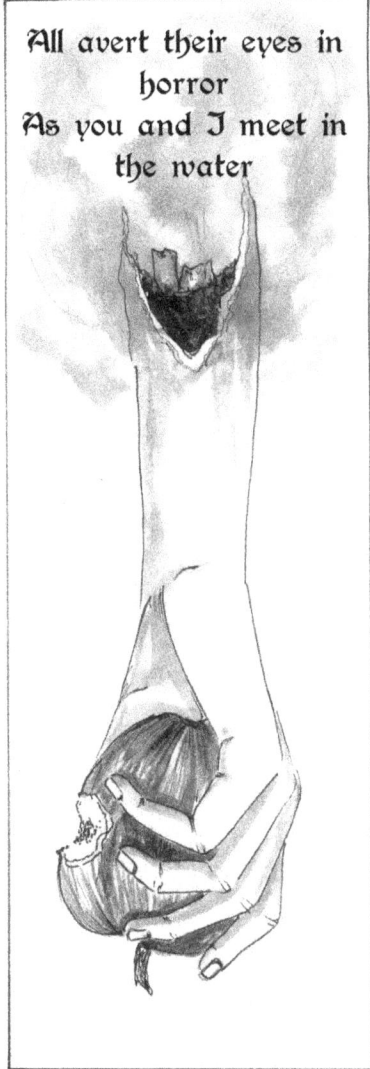

Nothing, Nevermore

I am hollow
I am hollow
My heart
It thumps against my chest
I am caving in
Just debris now on the floor
I am nothing, nevermore
Only dust now on the wind
Clinging desperately to your skin
To quote the raven "Nevermore"
For I am nevermore

I am hollow
I am hollow
My heart
It thumps against my chest
I am caving in
Just debris now on the floor
I am nothing, nevermore
Only dust now on the wind
Clinging desperately to your skin
To quote the raven "Nevermore"
For I am nevermore

My Fire

You're the one who lit

A thousand matches

And threw them on the pyre

Do not seem so shocked

When burnt by my fire

For one day I will burn in rage

And you'll burn in my ire

Remember twas you who stocked the flames

And raised them ever higher

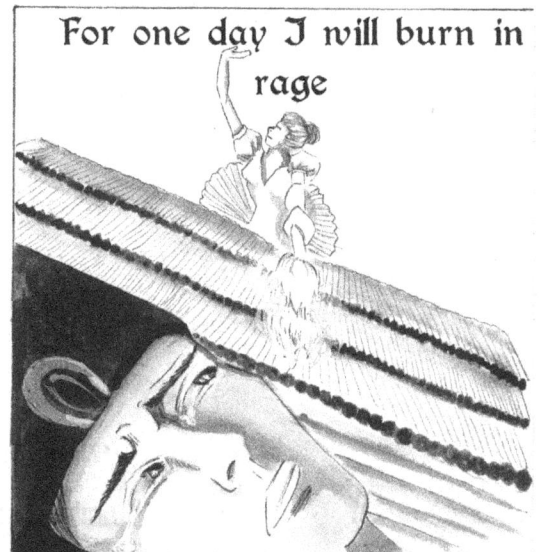

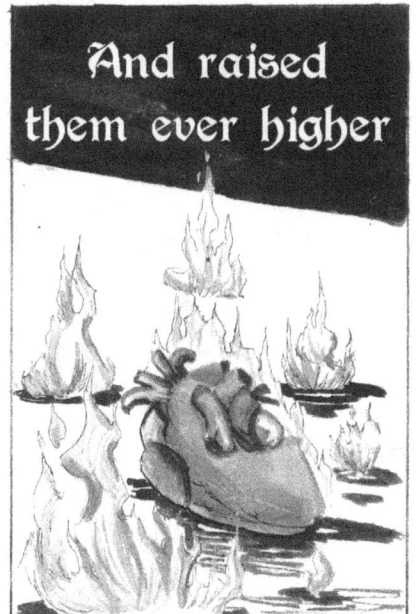

129

Hit The Ground

Hit the ground

Your face is plaster

Burned to ashes

All that surrounds you

Everyone

Nitroglycerine in your hands

Now it's your chance

As they explode in your nervous arms

Say your last words

You won't die soon

But everyone worth talking to

Has turned to soot in your hair

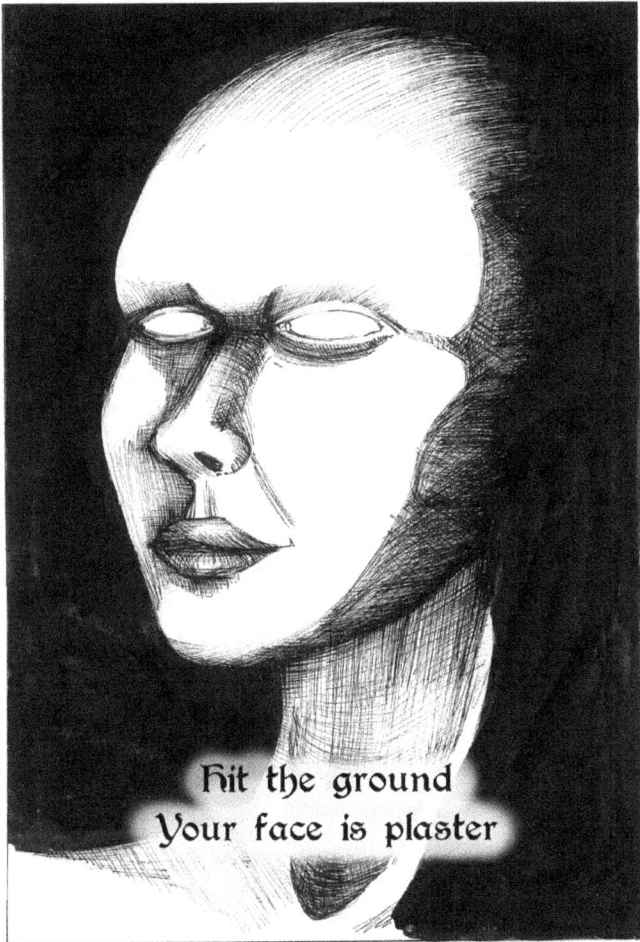

Hit the ground
Your face is plaster

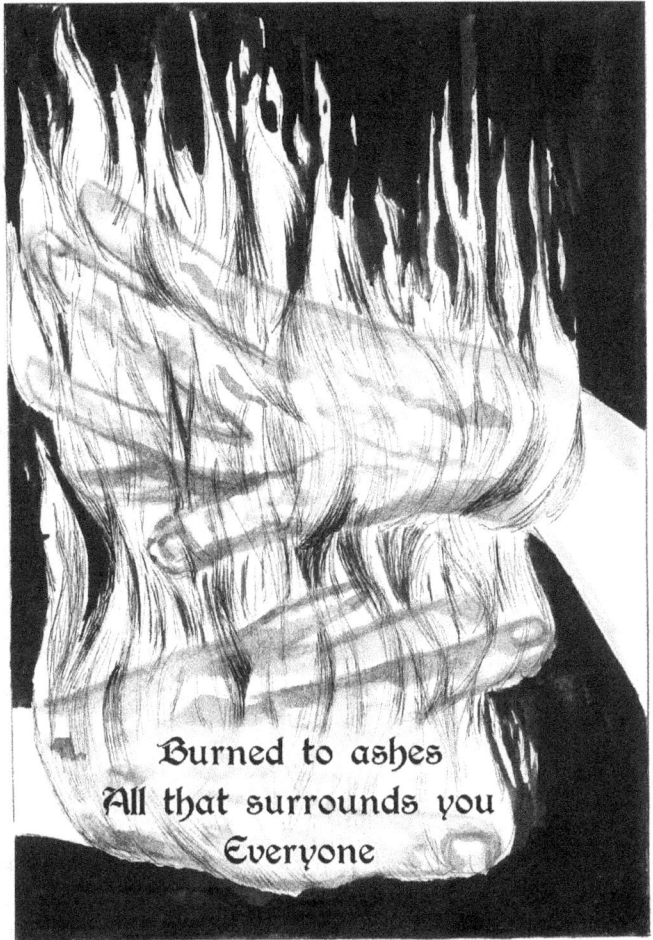

Burned to ashes
All that surrounds you
Everyone

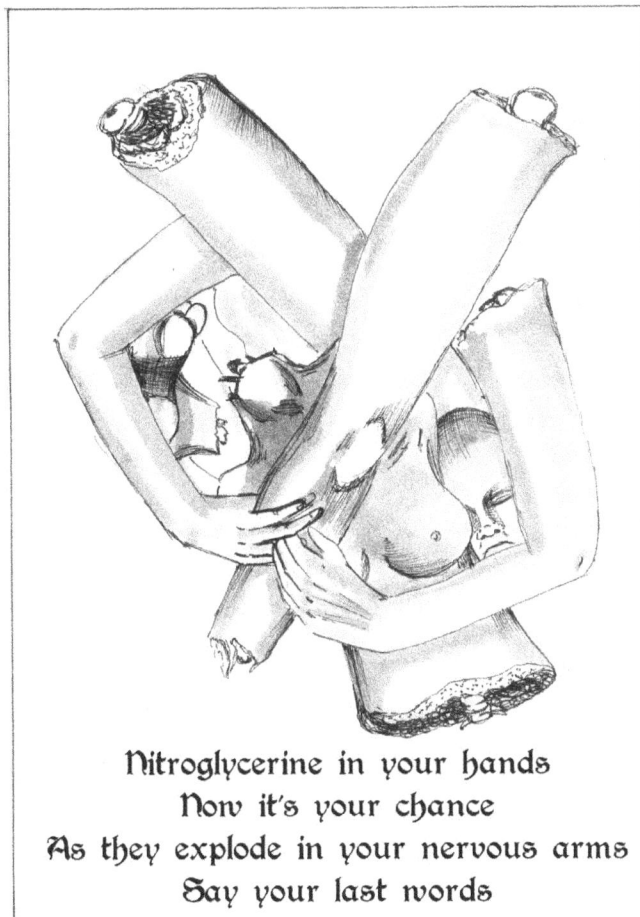

Nitroglycerine in your hands
Now it's your chance
As they explode in your nervous arms
Say your last words

You won't die soon
But everyone worth talking to
Has turned to soot in your hair

131

Caged

I rip my heart to shreds
In a fit of rage
As I'm soul repairing
My mind becomes a cage
I linger in a realm
Reality askew
And all I think is real
Insanity to you

I rip my heart to shreds
In a fit of rage
As I'm soul repairing
My mind becomes a cage

I linger in a realm
Reality askew
And all I think is real
Insanity to you

The Dragon

You'd left me bleeding
God Damn
I was pleading
The weakness inside me
You cultured and nourished
Thought you could
Collar and tame me
But it was
Your darkness
Your hellfire
That made me
Reach for a strength
I didn't know I possessed
And rise from these ashes
With rage in chest
To protect my child
As a dragon reborn
You cannot stand
Against the flame I exhale
Gone is the weakness
 you knew so well

You'd left me bleeding
God Damn

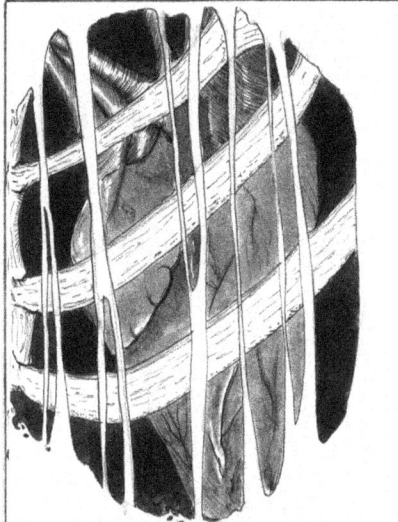

I was pleading
The weakness inside me
You cultured and
nourished

Thought you could
Collar and tame me

But it was
Your darkness
Your hellfire

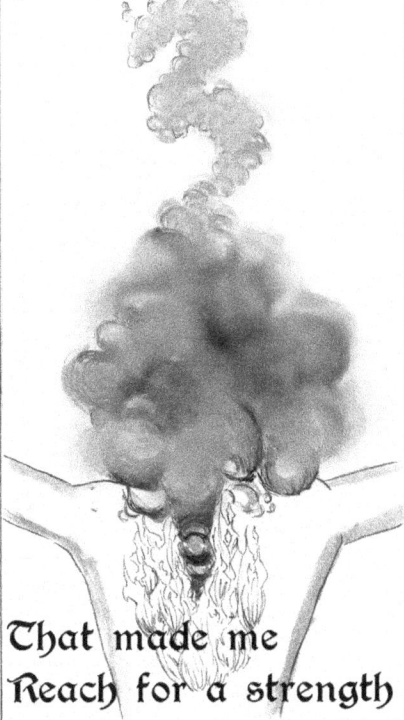

That made me
Reach for a strength

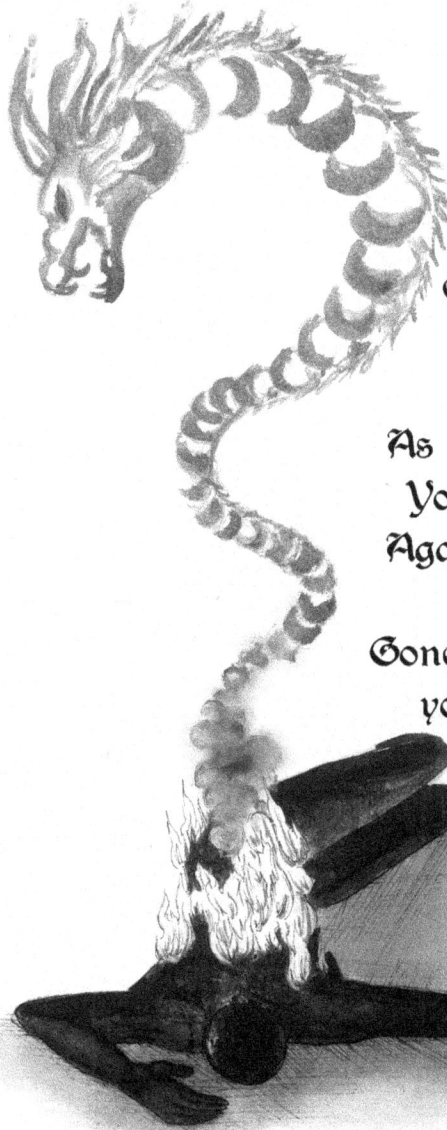

I didn't know I
possessed
And rise from
these ashes
With rage in chest
To protect my
child
As a dragon reborn
You cannot stand
Against the flame I
exhale
Gone is the weakness
you knew so well

The Soul King

Smells of burning rubber

For no isolated sin

Acrid his approach to tombs

Dwell in home the black and red

Weary as the bell tolls nine

I fear I have not left in time

There behold the jester himself

Painted red and grinning wild

Lo he tries to speak with me

Desperate as I am to flee

I am at root within the ground

"Your soul is safe for this day

I come for the one lying in the grave"

His spirit did then arise

From his newly dug house

Engulfed in chains that had no end

The jester opened his mouth wide

And condemned the soul to live inside

Pleas of thousands could be heard

As he tittered "I am the soul king."

Smells of burning rubber
For no isolated sin
Acrid his approach to tombs
Dwell in home the black and red
Weary as the bell tolls nine
I fear I have not left in time

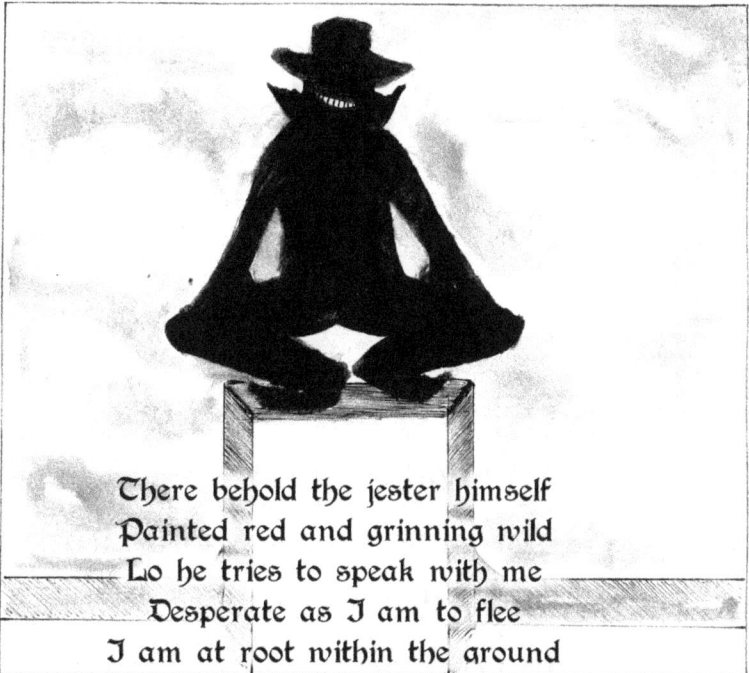

There behold the jester himself
Painted red and grinning wild
Lo he tries to speak with me
Desperate as I am to flee
I am at root within the ground

"Your soul is safe for this day
I come for the one lying in the grave."
His spirit did then arise
From his newly dug house
Engulfed in chains that had no
The jester opened his mouth wide
And condemned the soul to live inside
Pleas of thousands could be heard
As he tittered "I am the soul king."

Don't Presume

Object of my adoration

You walk a tightrope of deception

You abuse my giving nature

Never fearing repercussion

In your privileged place of heart

As you sit prideful

Take heed of my cautious tale

For you're close to my heart

but your tipping the scale

As you deceive and lie

You think my heart will deny

your actions

And act as a safe harbor for all of time

I suggest you look down, my sweet

At the thin wire you stumble across

High above the rest of the flock

At vertigo inducing height

And know that I see your deceptions

But listen and I'll tell you a story

One you'd be wise to take to heart
Once in God's loyal protection
The favored creation of his inception
Lucifer, beloved Morningstar
Held to the bosom of God
But Morningstar in his narcissistic arrogance
Thought to rise up above his maker
And though it sents God's heart to breaking
He banished his favored Morningstar
To a darkness devoid of Holiness, love, joy
He dared to presume
lest his prideful downward descent
For his crimes
Much like yours
there is no way
to repent
And if MorningStar could lose it all
Don't presume you cannot fall

Object of my
adoration
You walk a
tightrope of
deception

And act as a safe harbor for all of time
I suggest you look down, my sweet
At the thin wire you stumble across
High above the rest of the flock

You abuse my giving nature
Never fearing repercussion
In your privileged place of heart
As you sit prideful
Take heed of my cautious tale

For you're close to
my heart
but your tipping
the scale
As you deceive and lie
You think my heart will deny
your actions

At vertigo inducing height
And know that I see your deceptions
But listen and I'll tell you a story
One you'd be wise to to take to heart
Once in God's loyal protection

The favored creation of his
inception
Lucifer, beloved Morningstar
Held to the bosom of God

But Morningstar in his
narcistic arrogance
Thought to rise up
above his maker
And though it sets God's heart to
breaking

He banished his favored
Morningstar
To a darkness devoid of
Holiness, love, joy
He dared to presume
lest his prideful
downward descent
For his crimes
Much like yours

there is no way to repent
And if MorningStar could
lose it all
Don't presume you cannot fall

Broken Hearts

We've all got broken hearts
We loved each other so much
That we tore each other apart

Circle Of Earthly Remains

Circle of earthly remains
Embers ignite
In silent flames
Higher than the clouds collide
It rages on
Eclipilistic light

Broken Souls

A broken soul, like a shooting star, is a sight to behold with wonder
More akin to a meteor plummeting to earth.
Magnificent burning brightly, Fierce and Vibrant
And as the meteor crashes and smashed the earth beneath it, scorching its surroundings, so does the broken soul
But nothing is as enticing nor as beautiful to my eyes as a breaking spirit
No matter how oft they smash and scorch me still I seek them
For what a wonder
What a magnificent mystery
A puzzle I will always be drawn to put together
Alas, the missing and warped pieces, I cannot complete my work
The sphynx tells a riddle I cannot answer
The science of the soul
That is my work
For love is my nature
It is in my nature to love the monster for the man
Every shattered soul I touch tears at my own with a ferocious vibrancy
I give up those pieces of myself so eagerly
An addict
Getting high off the pain they supply
A broken soul myself
I shall try not to burn and smash you when hit the ground

A broken soul, like a shooting star, is a sight to behold with wonder
More akin to a meteor plummeting to earth.
Magnificent burning brightly.

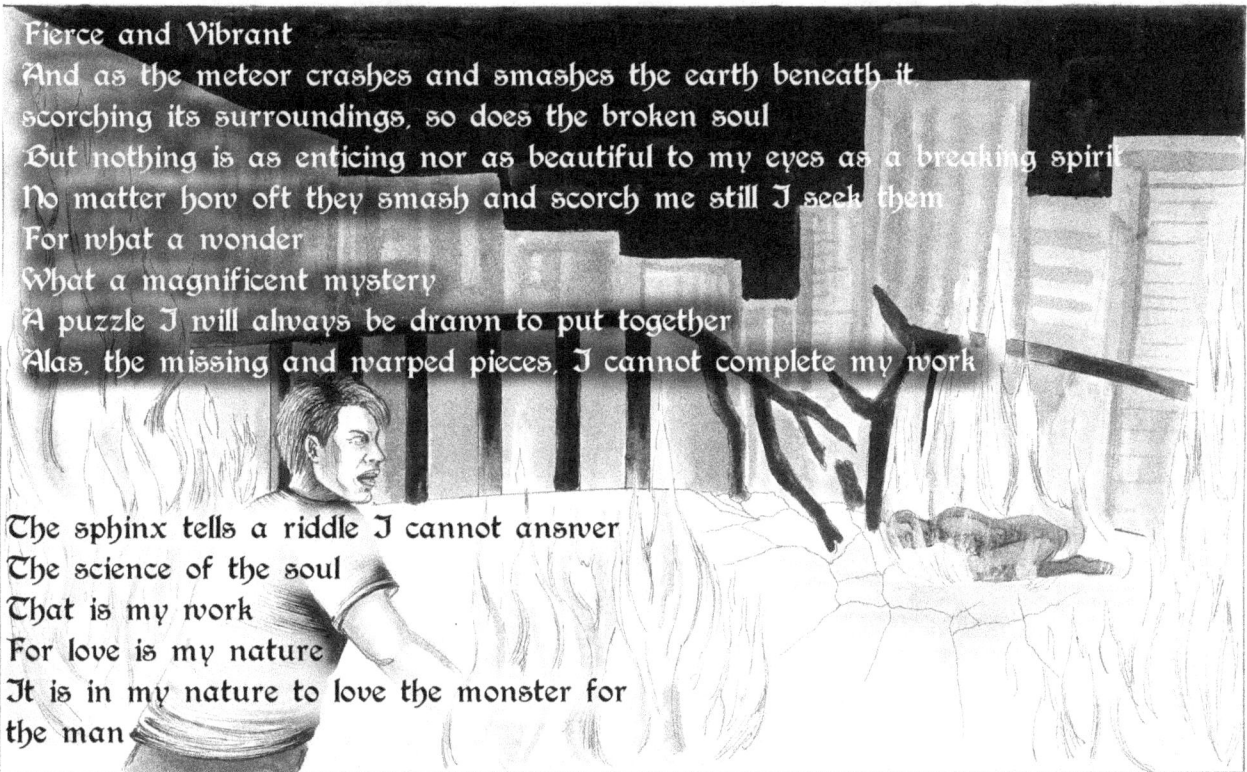

Fierce and Vibrant
And as the meteor crashes and smashes the earth beneath it
scorching its surroundings, so does the broken soul
But nothing is as enticing nor as beautiful to my eyes as a breaking spirit
No matter how oft they smash and scorch me still I seek them
For what a wonder
What a magnificent mystery
A puzzle I will always be drawn to put together
Alas, the missing and warped pieces, I cannot complete my work

The sphinx tells a riddle I cannot answer
The science of the soul
That is my work
For love is my nature
It is in my nature to love the monster for
the man

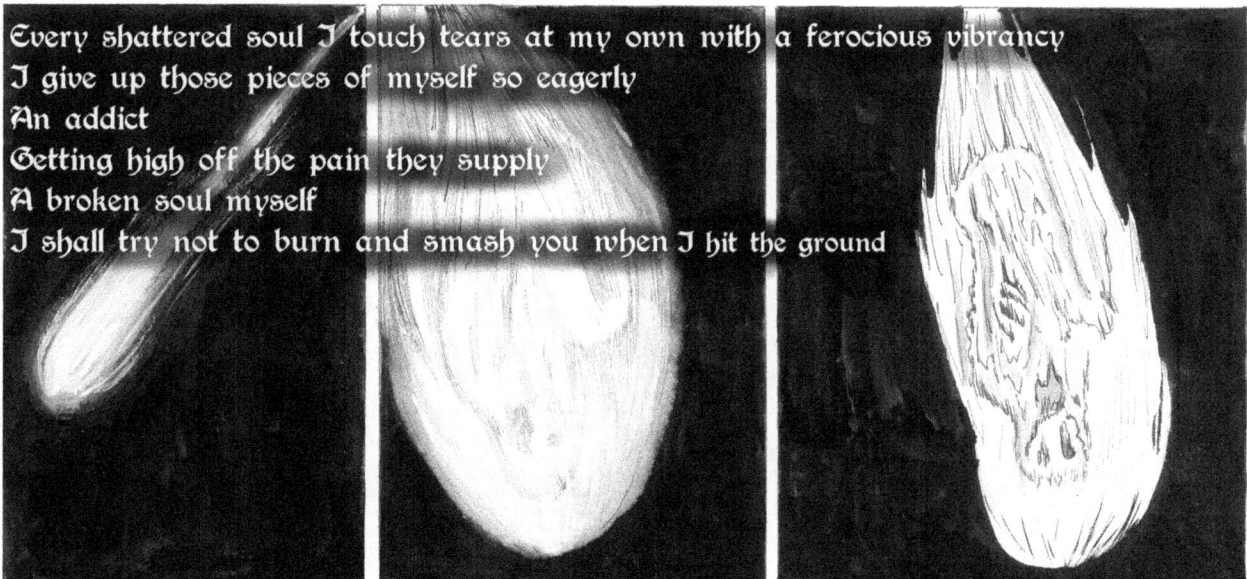

Every shattered soul I touch tears at my own with a ferocious vibrancy
I give up those pieces of myself so eagerly
An addict
Getting high off the pain they supply
A broken soul myself
I shall try not to burn and smash you when I hit the ground

www.ingramcontent.com/pod-product-compliance
Lightning Source LLC
Chambersburg PA
CBHW080115070426
42448CB00041B/3282